LITERACY CENTRE
Teacher's Resources

fiction yellow

Fantasy worlds

Hilary Braund, Deborah Gibbon
and Guy Merchant

CREDITS

Published by Scholastic Ltd,
Villiers House,
Clarendon Avenue,
Leamington Spa,
Warwickshire CV32 5PR

Printed by Ashford Colour Press Ltd,
Hants

© 2003 Scholastic Ltd
Text © 2003 Hilary Braund, Deborah Gibbon and Guy Merchant
1 2 3 4 5 6 7 8 9 0   3 4 5 6 7 8 9 0 1 2

SERIES EDITOR
Huw Thomas

SCOTTISH CONSULTANT
Sue Ellis (page 8)

AUTHORS
Hilary Braund, Deborah Gibbon and
Guy Merchant

EDITOR
Roanne Charles

ASSISTANT EDITOR
Dulcie Booth

SERIES DESIGNER
Joy Monkhouse

DESIGNER
Erik Ivens

ILLUSTRATIONS
Chris Riddell (pages 16, 27, 29; scans
from *Dreamboat Zing* pages 27, 34–5,
42–3)
Beverly Curl (pages 30, 58–9, 66–9, 81,
86, 88, 93–6, 108–9, 111–13, 116, 123)
David McKee (scan from *Zebra's Hiccups*
page 42)
Helen Cooper (pages 54, 61–3; scans
from *The baby who wouldn't go to bed*
pages 53, 55–6, 59, 71)
Jill Murphy (scans from *Whatever Next!*
pages 82–5, 89–90, 97–8)
Tony Ross (scans from *Dr Xargle's Book of
Earthlets* pages 108, 110–11, 114–15,
117, 124)
Carolyn Dinan (scans from *But Martin!*
pages 120, 122)

British Library Cataloguing-in-Publication Data
A catalogue record for this book is available from the British Library.

ISBN 0-590-53431-9

The rights of Hilary Braund, Deborah Gibbon and Guy Merchant to be identified as the Authors of this work has been asserted by them in accordance with the Copyright, Designs and Patents Act 1988.

ACKNOWLEDGEMENTS

The publishers wish to thank:
Andersen Press for the use of text and scanned illustrations from *Dr Xargle's Book of Earthlets* by Jeanne Willis, Text © 1988, Jeanne Willis, Illustrations © 1988, Tony Ross (1988, Andersen Press), and for text and illustration from *Zebra's Hiccups* by David McKee © 1991, David McKee (1991, Andersen Press); **Faber and Faber** for the use of an extract and scanned illustrations from *But Martin!* by June Counsel, Text © 1984, June Counsel, Illustrations © 1984, Carolyn Dinan (1984, Faber and Faber); **Macmillan Children's Books** for the use of text and scanned illustrations from *Whatever Next!* by Jill Murphy, Text and Illustrations © 1983, Jill Murphy (1983, Macmillan Children's Books, London); **The Penguin Group (UK)** for the use of text and scanned illustrations from *Dreamboat Zing* by Philip Ridley, Text © 1996, Philip Ridley, Illustrations (scans only) © 1996, Chris Riddell (1996, Puffin), line illustrations © 2003, Chris Riddell, previously unpublished; **Transworld Publishers, a division of The Random House Group Ltd** for the use of text and scanned illustrations from *The baby who wouldn't go to bed* by Helen Cooper, © 1996, Helen Cooper (1996, Doubleday), line illustrations © 2003, Helen Cooper, previously unpublished.

CONTENTS

CONTENTS

 # INTRODUCTION

Scholastic Literacy Centres are ready-made collections of quality children's literature put together by teachers for teachers. This resource helps teachers by:
■ selecting tried-and-tested children's books, each title chosen because it not only appeals to young readers but also draws out responses from them
■ supplying activities and information that help them to make the most of children's reading.

The teaching approach

This teacher's book has been structured to offer maximum flexibility for the various ways of working with books in today's classroom. It suggests:
■ ways to work with the whole class in shared reading
■ ways for setting up independent group work.

The approach makes books accessible to less confident readers through whole-class shared sessions, while allowing the more confident to read widely and respond at a deeper level to the books they read. The guided reading notes show teachers how to work through a book with a group of readers. The independent photocopiable pages, with their interactive style, foster reading independence in young readers and motivate them to read more widely.

The teacher's book gives opportunities for writing which build on reading, whether as a model for writing, or as a stimulus. It also suggests ways of linking reading and writing, building on teachers' experience and confidence in teaching reading, and extending these to teaching writing.

The photocopiable activities provide ample opportunities and forums for speaking and listening, whether in group discussion or in drama and role-play activities.

Selection of children's books

The children's books in each Literacy Centre resource a particular genre of fiction, non-fiction or poetry. Furthermore, they make particular reading demands on children, appropriate to the target age of each Centre. In these ways, the resource enables the books children read to work harder for teachers, allowing them to maximise the literacy and response potential of each one. Because each Centre is put together for a particular age group, progression is achieved from set to set. In addition, as the book selection in each Centre encompasses a range of reading abilities, progression is ensured within any particular set.

The core book and shared reading

Each Centre has a **core book** to be used with the whole class, either as a shared text or as a class reading book. It is chosen because:
■ it fits the range for the Centre
■ it will capture the imagination of children in the class
■ it can be used for whole-class teaching in a mixed-ability class

■ all children will be able to access the spirit of the book as well as mechanically decode it
■ it can be used to deliver the appropriate text-level literacy teaching objectives for the age group.

Three guided books

Each Centre has three **guided books** to be used for guided group reading. Like the core book, these books are chosen so that:
■ they fit the range for the Centre
■ they can be used to deliver the appropriate text-level literacy teaching objectives for the age group.

The three guided books plan for a range of abilities within a mixed-ability class and are selected for their differing reading demands:
■ one book is roughly equivalent to the reading level of the core book
■ one book is suitable for less confident readers
■ one book is suitable for more confident readers.

Teacher's resource book

In this resource book you will find four separate chapters of information and activities, corresponding to the four different children's books in the Centre. Each chapter contains:

■ information about the book, for example author notes, how it connects with sequels, background to the writing

■ guided reading notes indicating how the text can be read and re-read or split up over time – these may include questions that arise from the text, discussion points that emerge during reading, issues that focus the reader's attention, connections that can be made, and things that the children should look out for as they read the book

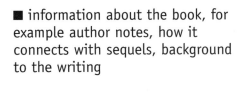

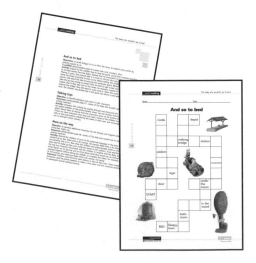

■ guided reading activities based on the book, plus linked photocopiables – these interactive activities, which further engage children in the book, are designed for independent group work; they keep children focused on the text and could include times when the guided reading groups split into pairs, make notes or do some guided writing

fiction yellow
Fantasy worlds

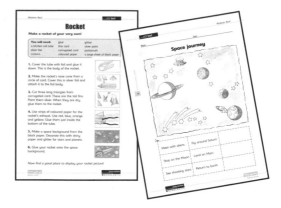

■ an extra photocopiable text, chosen because it links with and supports the book, for example a poem, a newspaper story or simply a montage of pictures – this has accompanying teacher's notes and three photocopiable activity sheets

■ two assessment photocopiables, with teacher's notes, each providing an activity to check children's knowledge of and response to the book; one of these should be done without access to the text.

SCHOLASTIC LITERACY CENTRES

The core book chapter

In addition to the above, the core book chapter has a shared reading section. The four shared texts (pages 15–18) give as many children as possible access to the core book through whole-class shared reading sessions. Drawn from the core book, the shared texts may include extracts, quotes, illustrations, selections of lines or dialogue. The shared texts are designed for photocopying onto A4 for individuals or pairs to read, or onto OHTs. They can also be enlarged to A3 for display.

Teachers should use the shared texts in the context of reading the book. How the teacher achieves this depends on the particular class: it may be that the teacher reads parts of the book to the class, or with a guided group or groups, or sets children to read independently in groups, in pairs or as individuals.

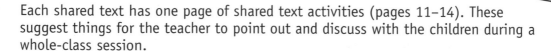

Each shared text has one page of shared text activities (pages 11–14). These suggest things for the teacher to point out and discuss with the children during a whole-class session.

Supplementary books

At the back of the book (pages 126–8) is a section of activity ideas for three supplementary books. Though not supplied as part of the Centre, the supplementary books link to the Centre's text range and teaching objectives, and are given here as suggestions for further widening the range of children's reading. One of the supplementary books suggested is intended to provide a particular reading challenge for the age group using the Centre.

fiction yellow

Fantasy worlds

Using Scholastic Literacy Centres in Scottish schools

The Scholastic Literacy Centres have been written to help schools build on the high standards for literacy that are being achieved in P1 and P2. They will be especially welcomed by schools and teachers who are looking for materials to develop a broad and robust programme for teaching and promoting literacy from P3 onwards. As part of such a programme, the Scholastic Literacy Centres can help raise standards by:

- ensuring progression and breadth in the reading material
- encouraging teachers to use the full range of classroom organisations and teaching techniques, selecting that which is most appropriate for the desired learning outcome
- ensuring that the reading–writing links are explicit so that children begin to use their experience as readers to inform their writing and to use their experience as writers to make them efficient and effective readers
- addressing the gender gap in reading by specifically targeting titles and activities which are exciting for both boys and girls
- introducing children (and teachers) to new authors and books, encouraging children to read a wider range of fiction and non-fiction for pleasure.

Teaching beyond the earliest stages of literacy

Schools which achieve high standards in literacy have teachers who:

- have high expectations and teach for success
- give literacy a high profile, ensuring that it is visible and part of the social currency in school
- are clear about the specific knowledge and skills children need to learn and have a good range of strategies for teaching them
- recognise the value of differentiation and group teaching but also use whole-class teaching and individual tasks effectively to achieve specific outcomes.

Scholastic Literacy Centres have been designed to promote such teaching. They offer a flexible, progressive framework for teaching literacy which fits perfectly with the approaches used in Scottish schools. The activities target all the Reading strands in the 5–14 Language Guidelines: 'Awareness of genre', 'Reading for information', 'Knowledge about language', 'Reading to reflect on the writer's ideas and craft', 'Reading aloud' and, of course, 'Reading for enjoyment'. The use of the texts as models and stimuli for writing allows teachers to cover key elements of teaching for the Writing strands 'Functional writing' and 'Imaginative writing'.

Organisation and teaching in the classroom

The quality of the texts and activities chosen for Scholastic Literacy Centres as well as the way in which it encourages good use of the teacher's time gives the very best support for developing a programme of work to help children become confident, fluent readers.

The **core book** provides a common literacy experience for the whole class. This ensures that children of all abilities learn to share and discuss key literacy issues and enables the teacher to both model and teach key ideas. Whole-class work, using the shared texts, develops the children's awareness of the different genres, promotes comprehension skills and highlights the craft of the writer as well as ensuring that the children are introduced to a broad range of fiction, poetry and information books.

The **guided books** can be used with ability groups to further develop these points. The children read texts closely matched to their reading abilities. They practise reading skills and learn to recognise and adopt appropriate reading behaviours for the different text organisations and purposes.

Finally, the **supplementary texts** guide teachers by suggesting books to further extend and develop particular interests and skills, helping to develop a rich and supportive literacy environment in the classroom.

QUICK GUIDE TO TEXTS AND LEVELS

Scholastic Literacy Centre Yellow Fiction:

Fantasy worlds

Section	Pages	Title	Approximate level of activities
Core book	10–36	*Dreamboat Zing* by Philip Ridley, illustrated by Chris Riddell	Level 1–2 Scottish Level A–B
Extra text for core book	37–42	*Zebra's Hiccups* by David McKee	Level 1–2 Scottish Level A–B
Guided book (equivalent level to core book)	45–63	*The baby who wouldn't go to bed* by Helen Cooper	Level 1–2 Scottish Level A–B
Extra text for guided book (equivalent level to core book)	64–9	Fantasy Island	Level 1–2 Scottish Level A–B
Guided book (less confident readers)	72–90	*Whatever Next!* by Jill Murphy	Level 1 Scottish Level A
Extra text for guided book (less confident readers)	91–6	Rocket	Level 1 Scottish Level A
Guided book (more confident readers)	99–117	*Dr Xargle's Book of Earthlets* by Jeanne Willis, illustrated by Tony Ross	Level 2 Scottish Level B
Extra text for guided book (more confident readers)	118–23	*But Martin!* by June Counsel, illustrated by Carolyn Dinan	Level 2 Scottish Level B
Supplementary books (more challenging)	126–8	*The Gruffalo* by Julia Donaldson, illustrated by Axel Scheffler *Where the Wild Things Are* by Maurice Sendak *Let the Lynx Come In* by Jonathan London, illustrated by Patrick Benson	

REAMBOAT ZING

BY PHILIP RIDLEY
ILLUSTRATED BY CHRIS RIDDELL

About the core book

Dreamboat Zing tells the story of a 'cool' creature with a seemingly incurable attack of hiccups. The creature is portrayed as a fantasy character living in an equally intriguing and fantastical land of caves, tropical islands and volcanoes. Dreamboat Zing is very vain and image conscious and likes to think that he is too cool to be scared. In fact, all his mother's attempts to scare away his hiccups *are* unsuccessful – until Dreamboat Zing catches an unflattering glimpse of himself in the mirror.

About the author and illustrator

Philip Ridley was born in east London in 1964. He has always enjoyed writing and completed his first novel by the age of seven. By the time he was fourteen, he had written about ten novels. As well as children's books, Philip Ridley writes for adults and has also written plays for radio and theatre, and film screenplays. However, he believes his writing for children is 'really the backbone of everything that I do'. His children's stories tend to have common themes of fears and fantasy, and he likes to explore issues such as family breakdown or bullying from a child's point of view. He has won awards for his novel *Krindlekrax* and been shortlisted for two further awards.

Chris Riddell was born in South Africa in 1962. He now lives in Brighton with his wife and three children. He has written and illustrated a number of children's books, including several prize-winning titles. As well as illustrating children's stories, Chris Riddell works as a cartoonist for several national newspapers.

Form and style

Dreamboat Zing is presented in a short novel format but makes use of repetition and patterned language typical of picture books. This, together with the many illustrations that intersperse the text, helps young children to confidently make the transition from picture books to a longer story.

The fantasy aspects of this story are provided by the setting, the appearance and unknown origin of the central characters and the improbable situations Mrs Zing puts them in, including surviving a volcanic eruption and being flown in the air by a hurricane. Nevertheless, readers are able to relate to and engage with the characters, as they will recognise the predicament of having hiccups and of being, or knowing, an image-conscious youngster with a 'helpful' parent.

The patterned language allows the children to build familiarity with the vocabulary as they read, while the repeated format and revision within the story lend themselves to a study of the structure and form of stories.

Looking at the front and back covers to introduce the book will encourage comments about the unusual figures, boat and building and offer opportunities for speculation on the content of the story and potential for exciting adventures for Dreamboat Zing.

Particularly cool

Background

This opening section of the story introduces the two central characters – Dreamboat Zing and his mother, Mrs Zing. Highlight and discuss the interesting structural point that here, unlike in many story openings we read, we are not given background information with regard to setting and character. The text reproduced here in isolation from Chris Riddell's illustrations doesn't confirm that Dreamboat Zing is a fantasy character, other than by his unusual name. Neither does it let us know where the story is set, although the facts that he is talking with his mother and looking in a mirror indicate that it is a domestic setting.

Focus on the characterisation of Dreamboat Zing and the children's personal responses towards him. At word level, encourage the children to look for and practise spelling patterns.

■ Read an enlarged copy of photocopiable page 15 out loud with the children. Ask them to recall from your earlier reading of the book where this section of text is taken from. If necessary, remind them that it is the very beginning of the story. Does the story begin in a way they would have expected? Ask what we learn about the story from this opening in terms of character, setting or content and compare it with other story beginnings they are familiar with.

■ Go on to talk further about content and how the opening of a story can often provide clues to what may happen in the rest of the story. Ask the children to use their knowledge of the book to identify any 'clues' given by the author in this opening passage. For example, Dreamboat Zing's statement that *nothing scares me* suggests that 'scary' things might happen to him later.

■ Focus on what Mrs Zing says to Dreamboat. Do the children know the meaning of *boast* and *admiring*? How do the children feel about what Dreamboat Zing has to say about himself? How could he describe himself without sounding as though he is boasting? (Point out the use of the word *so* which emphasises how he looks.)

■ Dreamboat Zing says that he is *cool*. What do the children think this means? From their suggestions, you should be able to develop a brief discussion on how the meaning is relative and may depend on whether you are a boy or a girl, and on how old you are.

■ Underline the letters *ea* in the first instance of *Dreamboat*. Help the children to identify and practise the sound made by this vowel digraph. Invite children to come up and underline any other examples of this letter combination that they can find within the extract (also in *clear, neat* and *clean*). Write all the words you have found on a large sheet of paper and display this in the classroom. Invite the children to add any other examples that they come across in their other reading.

SCHOLASTIC LITERACY CENTRES

Eeek!

Background

Children can often be unsure about moving on from picture books to attempting longer texts, particularly in the smaller, black and white, short novel format of *Dreamboat Zing*. By presenting these two extracts in close proximity, the patterned language and use of repetition within the structure of the story can be made explicit to the children and encourage them to tackle the reading independently and confidently.

Much of the story uses words that are not part of the children's high-frequency vocabulary, but the repetition within the story should help the children to recognise unfamiliar words on repeat and so broaden their vocabulary. The extracts given here can also be used to talk in more detail about the different frightening set-ups Mrs Zing provides for her son.

■ From your initial read-through of the book, ask the children if they can remember the four scenarios which Mrs Zing presented to Dreamboat Zing in her quest to scare him out of his hiccups. Show the children an enlarged copy of photocopiable page 16 and explain that it shows two extracts taken from those scenes. Read the first one to the children then invite them to help you read the second. Ask the children what they noticed about the text that helped them to join in with you as you read. Using a coloured pen, underline the words *explained Mrs Zing* in each extract. Then invite the children to use other colours to underline other words or phrases that are repeated across the two extracts.

■ Find the other two adventures in the book – where Mrs Zing takes Dreamboat to visit an erupting volcano and a hurricane-prone tropical island. Read out the passages from those scenes which reflect the two text extracts on photocopiable page 16. Ask the children to listen carefully to see if they can recognise any of the repeated phrases they have already identified on the enlarged sheet.

■ Talk about why Mrs Zing took Dreamboat to see the shark and the vampire bats. Make sure all of the children understand the common belief behind Mrs Zing's idea – that giving someone a fright or a shock will get rid of an attack of hiccups. Ask the children to identify what features or actions of the shark and the vampire bats were intended to scare Dreamboat. Do they think they would have been scared if they were in Dreamboat Zing's position?

■ Write the words *shark* and *vampire bats* on a flip chart or board. Surround each name with suggestions from the children of features they know about that creature. Encourage them to use information from the text as well as their own general knowledge. Then ask everyone if they believe all of the features to be true, for example that Great White sharks really like cheese and pickle sandwiches.

An ugly monster!

Background

In this passage, Dreamboat Zing sees himself for the first time after his adventures with his mother. He is so used to seeing himself looking neat and clean and 'cool' that he doesn't immediately recognise himself in his reflection. As Mrs Zing asks Dreamboat if he remembers how he came to look like that, this extract can be used as a prompt to encourage the children to recall from your initial reading of the book how his appearance changes due to events in the story.

This extract can be compared to the opening one, leading to a discussion of opposites and exploration of Dreamboat Zing's feelings about his appearance.

■ Enlarge photocopiable page 17 and ask the children to read the text with you. Discuss in particular the use of punctuation in this passage. Highlight all the exclamation marks used in Dreamboat Zing's speech. Can the children tell you why exclamation marks are used? Invite them to re-read the passage, using the expression suggested by the use of exclamation marks. Repeat this exercise, this time identifying the question marks used in Mrs Zing's parts of the conversation and again ask the children to read out her speech with appropriate expression.

■ At the end of the extract, Mrs Zing asks *'Don't you remember?'* as she explains to Dreamboat Zing why he now looks such a mess. Ask the children if they can remember how he came to have red eyes, messy hair, a dirty shirt and a shark's tooth around his neck.

■ Display the extract on photocopiable page 15 alongside this one. Explain to the children that both passages describe Dreamboat Zing's reaction as he looks in the mirror, but on different occasions. Ask them to describe Dreamboat Zing's appearance in the first extract and how he feels about himself. Then repeat this with the second extract. Ask the children to identify the opposites in the two extracts. For example, in the first description, Dreamboat Zing's eyes are clear, while in the second they are red. You may also want the children to make comparisons on the way the sentences are structured in the extracts – 'tidy', proper sentences in the first and short, 'scruffy' ones in the second.

■ Play a guessing game with the children. Invite one child to come out and give four clues to the identity of another child in the class, using a similar format to Dreamboat Zing's description of his reflection in the first extract. Write these four clues on the flip chart as the child gives them, for example *Her eyes are brown, her hair is long, she wears a blue shirt and lace-up shoes*. Invite the rest of the children to guess the identity of the child being described.

SCHOLASTIC LITERACY CENTRES

"Nothing scares me!"

Background

This text presents one complete scene from the story – Dreamboat and Mrs Zing's visit to a volcano. Revise and develop points that you have covered in studying the previous shared texts – the use of patterned language, Mrs Zing's intentions, how to use the punctuation to help understanding and in reading with expression. Draw the children's attention back to the fantasy element, including the lava-proof suits and Dreamboat Zing's lava slide. Discuss how Mrs Zing seems happy to put herself and her child in what we would consider extremely dangerous situations.

Work together to read the passage and highlight particular reading strategies and features of the text. This will help to build up the children's vocabulary and increase their confidence and ability to read the story independently.

■ Display an enlarged copy of photocopiable page 18, pointing out that it tells us what happened when Mrs Zing took Dreamboat Zing to see the erupting volcano. Underline these words on the page: *volcano, erupting, lava, erupted*. Ask if any of the children can read the words and help the volunteers where necessary. Explain that they may not be familiar with these words and that identifying and explaining them first will make it easier for them when they help you read the passage through. Check the children's understanding of the meaning of each of the words, then invite them to join in as you read the complete extract.

■ Remind the children of your earlier discussions regarding the use of exclamation marks and question marks in suggesting the tone of voice to be used when reading. Invite children to highlight all the exclamation marks and question marks within the extract. Then ask individual children to read sections of the text with suitable expression.

■ Ask the children if they think they would have been scared by being so close to an erupting volcano. Why do they think Dreamboat Zing was not scared? (Because he really *is* too cool?) Who ended up being scared in each of the adventures Mrs Zing organised for Dreamboat Zing?

■ Use the structure of this passage to retell one of the other scenes from the book. Remind the children that many of the phrases used here are repeated, or included in very similar ways, throughout the story (for example, *So Mrs Zing..., 'What are you doing?'* and *...and your hiccups will disappear*). Work orally to begin with. For example, in retelling the adventure in which Dreamboat and Mrs Zing meet the shark, the children may suggest, *So Mrs Zing took Dreamboat Zing out onto the ocean and threw cheese and pickle sandwiches in the water*. Explain that the retelling does not have to be a word perfect match to the way Philip Ridley has written it, but should use the structure of the original text. Invite the children to try this again with another of the adventures. This time, act as scribe for them and record their retelling on a flip chart or board.

Particularly cool

"I'm so cool," said Dreamboat Zing. "Nothing scares me."

"Don't boast," said his mother, Mrs Zing. "And stop admiring yourself in the mirror."

"But I'm so good-looking," said Dreamboat Zing.

"My eyes are so clear.
"My hair is so neat.
"My shirt is so clean.

"And the golden chain around my neck which says 'COOL' is particularly cool."

Philip Ridley

SCHOLASTIC LITERACY CENTRES

15

Eeek!

"The Great White shark adores cheese and pickle sandwiches," explained Mrs Zing. "When you see a shark's mouth full of a million sharp teeth, you'll be so scared, you'll go, 'Eeek!' and your hiccups will disappear."

"This cave is full of hungry vampire bats," explained Mrs Zing. "I'm going to burst the balloon to wake them up. When you see their flapping wings, you'll be so scared, you'll go, 'Eeek!' and your hiccups will disappear."

Philip Ridley

An ugly monster!

When they got home, Dreamboat Zing let out the loudest "Eeek!" Mrs Zing had ever heard.

"What's wrong?" she asked.

"An ugly monster!" Dreamboat Zing replied.

"It's got red eyes!

"Messy hair!

"A dirty shirt!

"And a sharp tooth around its neck! It scared me!"

"But it's just you in the mirror," Mrs Zing told him. "Don't you remember?"

Philip Ridley

"Nothing scares me!"

So Mrs Zing took Dreamboat Zing to a volcano and dressed them both in strange silver suits.

"What are you doing?" asked Dreamboat Zing. Then added, "Hic!"

"These silver clothes will protect us from the erupting volcano," explained Mrs Zing. "But when you see all that fire and lava, you'll be so scared, you'll go, 'Eeek!' and your hiccups will disappear."

Suddenly, the volcano erupted.

"Eeek!" went Mrs Zing.

But Dreamboat Zing just lay on a rock and let the stream of lava carry him down the side of the volcano.

"It's just like a big firework," he said. "And the silver clothes have messed up my hair – that's all! You see? Nothing scares me!"

Philip Ridley

GUIDED READING NOTES

Focus on page 3 of the book in which we are immediately introduced to Dreamboat Zing by his own description and Chris Riddell's illustration. Ask the children to share their impressions of Dreamboat Zing from his name, his appearance and his description of himself as being 'cool'. Have the children ever heard the expression 'dreamboat' before? What do they think it means? How do they think it applies to the character shown here?

Looking carefully at the illustration on page 3, talk about the story being a fantasy, based on bizarre and imaginary characters and, as is found out later in the story, impossible or improbable events. It may help to compare *Dreamboat Zing* with

a familiar story that draws inspiration from real life. Compare characters, names, settings and events to highlight the strange and completely imaginary aspects of fantasy worlds.

Read on together up to page 7. Ask the children to find the section of text where Mrs Zing tells Dreamboat off for boasting (page 4). On the flip chart, write the words *boastful* and *cool*. Tell the children that these are two words that can be used to describe Dreamboat Zing from different points of view (his mother's and his). Talk about some of the things he does and ask the children to decide if his actions are boastful or cool, giving reasons. Ask them to suggest a range of other words that could be used to describe him and add these to the list started on the flip chart, for example *trendy*, *show-off*, *vain*, *fun*. Using two different-coloured pens, ask the children to highlight the words to show which Dreamboat might use about himself and which might be used by Mrs Zing.

Read pages 8–11. Discuss how the two characters feel about Dreamboat Zing having the hiccups. Is Mrs Zing sympathetic? Is Dreamboat Zing grateful for his mother's suggestion of help?

Mrs Zing says she only knows of one cure for hiccups. Ask the children if they know of any others. Suggest that they make a collection of hiccup 'cures' by talking to other children and adults around the school. Ideas collected may include drinking a glass of water 'upside down', putting something cold down your back and holding your breath and counting to ten. Consider which of the cures would work for Dreamboat Zing. Are there any he would be too cool to try or which even Mrs Zing might think too dangerous? The group could then work together to make a small illustrated booklet of cures. Ask them to suggest a suitable title, such as *Dreamboat Zing's Little Book of Hiccup Cures*.

CONT. . .

CONT...

20

Read pages 12–29. You may like to begin this longer session by asking individual children to read sections of the text out loud, inviting help from the rest of the group if necessary. As you reach the second complete scene where the pattern of the language and repetition becomes obvious (page 23), you might feel you could ask the children to read on independently up to page 29. Encourage them to read silently or very quietly to themselves. When the group have completed the reading of this whole section of text, talk about the repetition within the story. Ask the children to identify phrases that they recognise as being repeated, and write these up on the flip chart. Reinforce the children's appreciation of how this use of patterned language assists the reader, especially when dealing with new vocabulary, and also adds enjoyment through consistency, familiarity and the anticipation of what comes next.

As well as focusing on the repetition within the use of vocabulary, identify the repetition of similar events – Mrs Zing taking Dreamboat Zing on an adventure somewhere to frighten his hiccups away, Dreamboat Zing hiccuping after asking *'What are you doing?'*, Mrs Zing being scared while her son is not, and so on.

Read together the text on page 30. Explain to the children that they are going to attempt to read the next section of the book independently. But first they are to use their knowledge of repeated events and phrases to give you as much detail as they can about the rest of this scene and the language used, without looking at the text. You could write some of their suggestions on the flip chart, for example *The silver clothes protect them from the fire and lava* and *'Eeek!' went Mrs Zing.*

By focusing on the vocabulary used and the sequence of events, the children should be able to read up to page 39 confidently on their own. When they have finished reading, return to the suggestions that you wrote on the flip chart in the previous session. Ask the children if they would now want to change the vocabulary used or the order of the words that they had previously supplied. Make these changes on the flip chart and while doing so ask whether the changes have made any difference to the meaning or the nature of the events that they had recalled. This can lead to a discussion about how the same meaning can be presented in different ways just by changing the order of the words or the vocabulary used.

Ask the group if they can recall the final destination for Dreamboat and Mrs Zing. Turn to page 40 and ask the children to read on until page 53. When they have finished reading, ask them to identify what happened in this scene. Highlight (orally) some of the more difficult words used to ensure all of the children can make sense of the vocabulary. Ask what they know about 'tropical' islands and in particular hurricanes. Have they seen footage of them on the news or read about them in books or newspapers? Would flying a kite really be possible in a hurricane, or is it a fantasy?

Examine the text and illustration on page 53. In some ways it looks and sounds like the end of the story. Ask the children what particular features remind them of a story ending (particularly the way we see the characters from behind, looking out towards the boat as though everything is over, and that Mrs Zing suggests going home). Continue this discussion by asking why this would not be a satisfactory ending for the story. What issues are still to be addressed and what aspects of the story still need to be brought to a satisfactory conclusion? (Dreamboat Zing still has hiccups. How is he going to react when he sees himself in the mirror when he gets home?)

Read from page 54 to the end of the book. You may like to read out loud all together or ask the children to take turns in reading a page each, helping them where necessary. Then go back to look at the illustrations on pages 54–9. Explore how they show changes in both Dreamboat Zing's appearance and attitude, for example he no longer seems confident and 'cool', instead, by the end of the sequence he is clutching onto his mother.

Ask the children to tell you what happened at the very end of the story. Recap on the words you collected to describe Dreamboat Zing in the first guided reading session (see page 19), and ask the children to suggest words to describe Dreamboat Zing as he is at the end, for example *kind*, *helpful* and probably *grateful* to his mother.

Having now read the whole story, ask the children to consider what Dreamboat Zing may have learned from his adventures. Mrs Zing's intention was to scare away the hiccups, which ultimately she achieved, but did Dreamboat Zing gain anything else from his adventures and their consequences? For example, will he be less concerned with the way he looks and more helpful to his mother?

ACTIVITY NOTES

Scaring away hiccups

Objectives: to recall events from the story; to use imagination to create alternative events.

Resources: photocopiable page 26, copies of *Dreamboat Zing*, writing and drawing materials.

Activity: Read through the headings at the top of the chart and the example in the first row. Explain to the children that to complete the next three rows, they should use the book to help them recall the other ways in which Mrs Zing tried to scare Dreamboat Zing out of his hiccups, drawing the 'scare factor' if they wish. Then encourage the children to invent their own 'scary' fantasy adventure that might help to cure Dreamboat Zing and use this idea to fill in the last row.

How did it happen?

Objective: to use recall of the story to match cause and effect.

Resources: photocopiable page 27, paper, scissors, glue.

Activity: Discuss with the children how Dreamboat Zing looked by the end of the story and recall the four particular changes to his appearance that made him look such a mess. Identify the four illustrations on the sheet that show these changes, and read through the speech bubbles together. Explain that the four remaining illustrations and captions show what had happened to Dreamboat Zing to result in him looking like an *ugly monster*. Ask the children to cut out all of the sections, match each event with the appropriate change in Dreamboat Zing's appearance and glue the matching pairs together onto a separate sheet of paper.

Extension: Ask the children to create a third illustration to go with each matching pair that shows an earlier stage of the adventure Dreamboat Zing underwent, leading to the illustrated event and the change in his appearance. For example, the children could draw a picture of Dreamboat Zing being whisked into the air to accompany the illustration of him covered with flowers and with red eyes.

Another fright

Objective: to use their own ideas to write using the repetitive format of the story.

Organisation: photocopiable page 28, writing materials.

Activity: Recap on your previous discussions regarding the repeated structure and phrases used in the story. Refer to the lists of repetition that you collected during the shared and guided reading activities (see pages 14 and 20). Read through the photocopiable sheet with the group. Explain that it gives all the repeated phrases from the four adventures that the characters encounter, but the details have been left out. Ask the children to come up with their own ideas of how to scare the hiccups from Dreamboat Zing and to use these ideas to complete the page. Remind the children of the suggestions they thought of when completing the first activity, 'Scaring away hiccups' on page 26.

Opposites

Objective: to identify instances of opposites in the story.

Resources: photocopiable page 29, copies of *Dreamboat Zing*, writing and drawing materials.

Activity: Ask the children to look at the contrasting pictures of Dreamboat Zing on pages 6 and 54 of the book. Discuss the images and ask the children to make comparisons between different aspects of his clothes and appearance. Establish the meaning of the word *opposite* and focus on aspects of the pictures that illustrate opposites. Ask the children to write and illustrate the opposites to complete the table on the photocopiable sheet. (There is space in the table for the children to include Dreamboat Zing's necklace if they want to, which 'changed' from being cool to being scary, but is not strictly an opposite.)

Dear Sally

Objective: to write in the style of a problem page, drawing ideas from the story.

Resources: photocopiable page 30, copies of *Dreamboat Zing*, writing materials, problem pages from children's magazines (optional).

Activity: Ask the children if they have ever heard of or read a problem page. If necessary, explain that it is a feature of some magazines to which people write for solutions to various, usually personal, problems and the magazine prints helpful advice in reply from its 'agony aunt'. Show the children a couple of examples if you have them, particularly the replies, to help the children get an idea of the style of writing. Together, read through the letter to 'Sally' from Dreamboat Zing. Suggest to the children that they use ideas from the story or from earlier discussions about hiccup cures to write a reply to Dreamboat Zing. Explain that they should focus on just one or two suggestions and think carefully about how they finish their reply, giving hopeful advice and good wishes.

Pair them up

Objective: to recognise and complete sentences and events from the story.

Resources: copies of photocopiable page 31, writing materials, scissors, glue, paper.

Activity: Explain to the children that the photocopiable sheet shows four sentence beginnings and endings from *Dreamboat Zing* and that their task is to pair them up to create complete sentences as they appeared in the story. Invite the children to check their understanding by reading through all of the sentence sections before they start cutting them out. Ask the children to paste the correct sentence ending beneath each sentence beginning, then read each complete sentence through again to check.

Extension: Ask the children to make up their own page of split sentences using the text on pages 49–52, for example *Not a shark... ...with a million sharp teeth*. The page could then be given to a friend to complete.

Find the word

Objectives: to read a passage from the book, identifying missing words; to recognise the suffix *ed*.

Resources: photocopiable page 32, copies of *Dreamboat Zing*, writing materials.

Activity: Ask the children what they notice about the passage of text on the photocopiable sheet. Look at the words at the bottom of the page and discuss what they all have in common. Explain how the *ed* ending indicates a past-tense form of a verb. Read through the passage with the group, inviting children to suggest what the missing words should be. Encourage them to have a go at working out what a word might be from the sense of the surrounding sentence. Then ask the children to complete the text independently. Advise them to look through pages 43–8 of *Dreamboat Zing* to check their work once they have finished.

Extension: Ask the children to scan through the book and list any other words ending in *ed* that they come across.

Mix and match

Objective: to use recall to match and group words from the story.

Resources: photocopiable page 33, paper, scissors, glue, writing and drawing materials.

Activity: Ask the children if they can read the words on the photocopiable sheet. Work together to identify all of the words. Explain to the children that you want them to group the sets of *three* words or phrases that go together in the context of the adventures in *Dreamboat Zing*, for example *volcano*, *silver suits* and *fire and lava*. Ask the children to cut out the words and phrases from the photocopiable sheet and glue them together on the plain paper. They can choose their own method of presentation. Then ask them to illustrate one or more of the adventures.

Extension: Ask the children to choose one set of words or phrases and use it to make a sentence explaining what happened in that part of the story, for example *Dreamboat Zing and Mrs Zing wore silver suits when they went to the volcano to protect them from the fire and lava.*

Dreamboat Zing's guide to being cool

Objective: to write captions using recall of the story and their imaginations.

Resources: photocopiable page 34, writing materials.

Activity: See what the children remember about the features of Dreamboat Zing's appearance that he believed made him 'cool'. (For example, his eyes, hair and shirt.) After this discussion, ask the children to add captions to the diagram on the photocopiable sheet. If necessary, remind the children how the text in guides like this is written – as positive instructions. Encourage the children to make their captions as imaginative and descriptive as possible, for example *Make sure your shirt is perfectly clean and without creases.*

Not so cool

Objectives: to recall details from the story; to explore the drafting process through shared writing.

Resources: photocopiable page 35, paper, writing materials.

Activity: Show the children the illustration on the sheet showing Dreamboat Zing when he had completed his adventures. Point out the labelled features and ask the children to remember how each came about. With you or one of the group as scribe, create some shared writing, recalling each incident and the effect it had on Dreamboat Zing's appearance. (For example, *Mrs Zing took Dreamboat Zing to a tropical island. The hurricane whisked him and his kite into the air. When he landed, he got covered in flowers which gave him hay fever. This made his eyes red.*) Begin the writing on a separate sheet of paper so you can model how to redraft it in response to different ideas or to improve the range of vocabulary or punctuation used. When the group are happy with the composition for each feature, it can be written carefully around the picture by you or the scribe.

Dreamboat words

Objectives: to extend vocabulary; to practise word-level strategies.

Resources: photocopiable page 36 copied onto card and cut into individual word cards, copies of *Dreamboat Zing*, A3 paper, dictionaries (optional).

Activity: Explain that you are going to be looking at some of the more difficult words in the story. Place the cards face down and invite one of the children to pick a card, turn it over and attempt to read the word. Encourage the rest of the group to help if appropriate. Talk through the strategies we can use to read the word, including identifying sounds within the word, noticing any similarity with known words or remembering it from the story. Turn to the page number shown on the card and ask the children to find the word in the text. Show how reading a word in context helps when reading less familiar vocabulary. Repeat the activity with the other word cards.

Ask the children if they can tell you the meaning of any of the words. On a large sheet of paper, work with the group to write definitions of each word. You may like to show them how a dictionary can help in finding the definitions of words.

Danger

Objective: to identify the dangerous aspects of each adventure in the story.

Resources: A3 paper, writing and drawing materials.

Activity: Divide the paper into four sections. Explain to the group that they are going to work together to create a large picture showing the four adventures undertaken by Mrs Zing and Dreamboat Zing. Divide the group into four and position the children around the large sheet of paper so they can all work at the same time, each smaller group creating one of the four illustrations. Make sure they leave enough space for a danger sign in each section. While they are working, cut out four large paper signposts, labelled at the top with *DANGER*. Once the illustrations are finished, work as a group to complete each danger sign with a caption telling of the hazard in each picture and what to do about it, for example *DANGER – Great White shark. NO SWIMMING!*, and attach these to the pictures.

Name   Date

Scaring away hiccups

Setting	Scare factor	What happened
the ocean	Great White shark	The shark bit off Dreamboat Zing's necklace. Dreamboat Zing pulled out one of the shark's teeth.

Name   Date

How did it happen?

My eyes are red.

My hair is a mess.

My shirt is dirty.

There's a sharp tooth round my neck.

Dreamboat Zing wore some silver clothes.

The bats' wings tickled Dreamboat Zing.

Dreamboat Zing pulled a tooth from the shark's jaws.

Dreamboat Zing was covered in flowers.

fiction yellow

Fantasy worlds

photocopiable

SCHOLASTIC

Name _____   Date _____

Another fright

So Mrs Zing took Dreamboat Zing to _____

_____

_____

"What are you doing?" asked Dreamboat Zing. Then added,

"Hic!"

"_____

_____,"

explained Mrs Zing. "_____

_____,

you'll be so scared, you'll go, 'Eeek!' and your hiccups will

disappear."

Suddenly, _____

_____

"Eeek!" went Mrs Zing.

But Dreamboat Zing just _____

_____

_____

"You see? Nothing scares me!"

Name _____   Date _____

Opposites

Beginning of the story	**End of the story**
	messy hair
a clean shirt	

SCHOLASTIC LITERACY CENTRES

Name   Date

Dear Sally

Dear Sally,
I hope you can help me. I have a bad case of the hiccups and it is ruining my image. My mum says they make me look funny and shake like a jelly. I usually look really cool. Have you any ideas for getting rid of hiccups?

Thank you
from Dreamboat Zing

Dear Dreamboat Zing,
Sorry to hear you have the hiccups. I can understand how they might spoil your cool image.

Name _____   Date _____

Pair them up

So Mrs Zing rowed Dreamboat Zing to the middle of an ocean

```



```

So Mrs Zing took Dreamboat Zing to a big, dark cave

```



```

So Mrs Zing took Dreamboat Zing to a volcano

```



```

SCHOLASTIC LITERACY CENTRES

So Mrs Zing took Dreamboat Zing to a tropical island

```



```

✂ -

and started to blow up a balloon.

and handed him a kite.

and started throwing cheese and pickle sandwiches into the water.

and dressed them both in strange silver suits.

fiction yellow
Fantasy worlds

■ SCHOLASTIC

Name _____   Date _____

Find the word

"There'll be a hurricane soon," _____

Mrs Zing. "When the wind whisks you into the air and

you see tropical trees _____ and whirling

around you, you'll be so scared, you'll go, 'Eeek!' and

your hiccups will disappear."

Suddenly, a hurricane _____ them

into the air.

"Eeek!" went Mrs Zing.

But Dreamboat Zing just _____ the

view. "It's like a roller-coaster ride!" he said.

When he _____ he was

_____ in flowers. "These things have

brought on my hay fever and made my eyes red

– that's all!"

admired	explained	landed
covered	whisked	uprooted

fiction **yellow**

Fantasy worlds

Name   Date

Mix and match

tropical island

volcano

cave

Great White
shark

hurricane

silver suits

kite

vampire bats

ocean

cheese and pickle
sandwiches

balloon

fire and lava

Name

Date

Dreamboat Zing's guide
to being cool

Make sure your shirt is

SCHOLASTIC

fiction **yellow**
Fantasy worlds

Name

Date

Not so cool

Red eyes

Messy hair

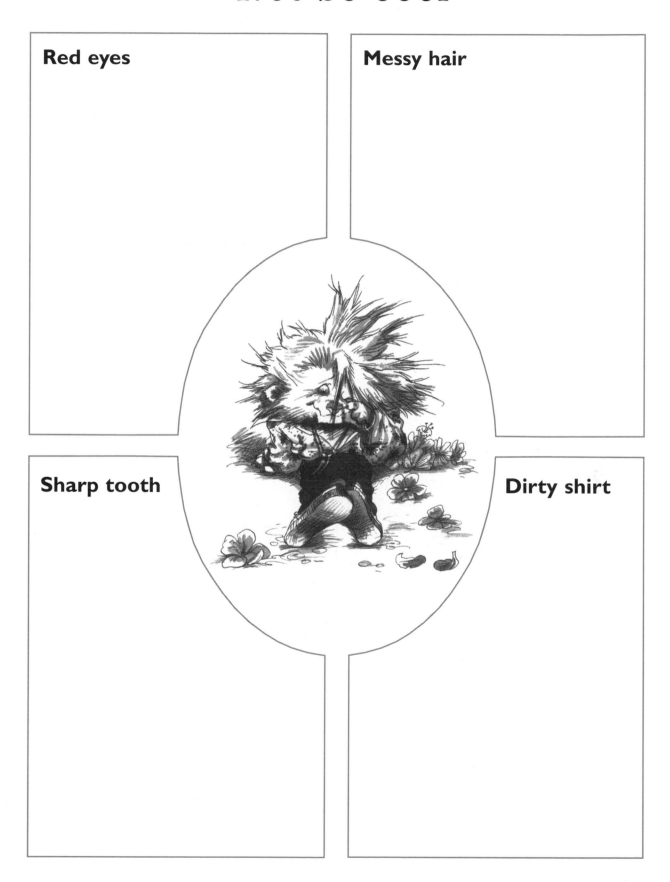

Sharp tooth

Dirty shirt

Name   Date

Dreamboat words

exclaimed 8	ocean 12
merely 18	vampire 23
suddenly 26	volcano 30
erupting 33	tropical 40
hurricane 43	whisked 44
particularly 7	admiring 4

Zebra's Hiccups

Background

This text is the beginning of the story *Zebra's Hiccups* by David McKee. The complete story goes on to tell how the hiccups eventually result in Zebra's stripes joining up, so making him look ridiculous. He is forced to swallow his pride and try out the *far too un-HIC dignified* cures suggested to him by the animals. In the end, the hiccups are cured by Zebra being given a shock as the animals shower him in cold water.

Highlight the clear parallels with *Dreamboat Zing*. Both central characters are aloof and very concerned with their appearance, and become worried that having the hiccups will ruin their image. A number of hiccup cures are suggested, although in *Dreamboat Zing* they are all based on giving him a fright. Finally, both characters are cured of hiccups by receiving a shock.

■ Enlarge the extract on photocopiable page 39 and display it where the children can read it. Ask the children to read the title with you, and ask them how they think this story links with *Dreamboat Zing*.

■ Read the text out loud as far as *Perhaps they will disappear*, near the middle. Ask the children what they have learned about Zebra from this introduction. Do they think Zebra is a similar character to Dreamboat Zing in any way?

■ Read the rest of the text out loud, explaining any vocabulary the children may not understand. Ask them whether the hiccup cure offered by Zebra has come up in their previous discussions about suggested cures. Ask why they think Zebra was unwilling to give it a try.

■ Tell the children that, in the rest of the story, the hiccup cures offered to Zebra become increasingly silly, and give them some examples: Miss Pig suggests he puts his head between his knees and drinks a glass of water upside down, Little Elephant says that what he does when he suffers an attack of hiccups is stand on one leg and sing a special song. Ask the children to work in pairs to think of their own ridiculous cures, rather than the more sensible ones that people do try as included in earlier discussions (see page 19). Ask the children to write their ideas on photocopiable page 40 and to draw pictures of themselves trying each one.

■ Make an enlarged copy of photocopiable page 41. Explain to the children that you are going to work together to imagine, plan and then write about Zebra's next encounter with one of the animals. Use the boxes at the top of the page to make notes on the character he meets, the cure he or she suggests and Zebra's response. Share some of the cures invented for photocopiable page 40 and choose a favourite of these as an example. Then, with the children's help, write a continuous passage for the story, using a similar structure to that in the extract on photocopiable page 39. Give out individual copies of the sheet and ask the children to complete their own page using their own ideas.

CONT. . .

SCHOLASTIC LITERACY CENTRES

CONT. . .

■ Divide the children into two groups and give each group a copy of photocopiable page 42. Explain that one group is going to look at the similarities and differences in the beginnings of *Dreamboat Zing* and *Zebra's Hiccups* and the other group will compare the central characters. Ask one child from each group to scribe, explaining that where the two circles overlap, they should write about things that are the same for both stories. For example, both characters have hiccups, both are very aware of their appearance and image. When the children have finished, ask the groups to swap their sheets and see if they can add anything more.

■ Ask the children what they think happens next in the story, and how they think it might end. After they have given some suggestions of their own, tell them the remainder of the story as described in the 'Background' section and the notes for photocopiable page 40. Ask the children what lesson they think Zebra learned from his experience of having hiccups, and compare this with the discussion they had about Dreamboat Zing (see page 21).

assessment

ASSESSMENT NOTES

Mrs Zing or Dreamboat Zing?

Assessment focus: to use knowledge of the two central characters to identify and match spoken phrases from the story.
Resources: photocopiable page 43, coloured writing materials.
Activity: Ask the children to read the spoken phrases on the photocopiable sheet. Explain that using their knowledge of the story and the characters, they should draw a line matching each phrase to the character that said it. Suggest that they use a different colour for each character.

Make the story

Assessment focus: to read extracts taken from the story and order them in the correct sequence; to put phrases together to form sentences.
Resources: copies of photocopiable page 44, scissors, glue, paper.
Activity: Explain to the children that the text on the photocopiable sheet makes up one of the adventures from *Dreamboat Zing*, but that the sentences and phrases are not in the right order. Ask the children to cut out the strips of text and arrange them on the plain paper in the correct order. Advise them to read the whole piece through before gluing the strips in place.

Zebra's Hiccups

The animals loved to play.

"Come and play, Zebra," they called. "This is fun."

"No thank you, I am busy," Zebra answered. He was a very serious and dignified zebra.

One day, Zebra got hiccups.

"Oh my, how extremely inconvenient HIC," he said to himself. "I shall simply, HIC, ignore them and go out for a walk. Perhaps they will disappear."

"Hi there, Zebra," said Tiger.

"Good HIC, ah. Good morning HIC," said Zebra.

"Hiccups!" said Tiger. "Don't worry I know a cure. Hold your breath, close your eyes, and say the alphabet backwards."

"That sounds much too HIC silly," said Zebra.

David McKee

Name

Date

Hiccup cures

fiction **yellow**

Fantasy worlds

Name _____ Date _____

A cure for Zebra

Animal	Hiccups cure

Zebra's response

_____

_____

_____

_____

_____

_____

Name

Date

The same but different

Zebra's Hiccups

Dreamboat Zing

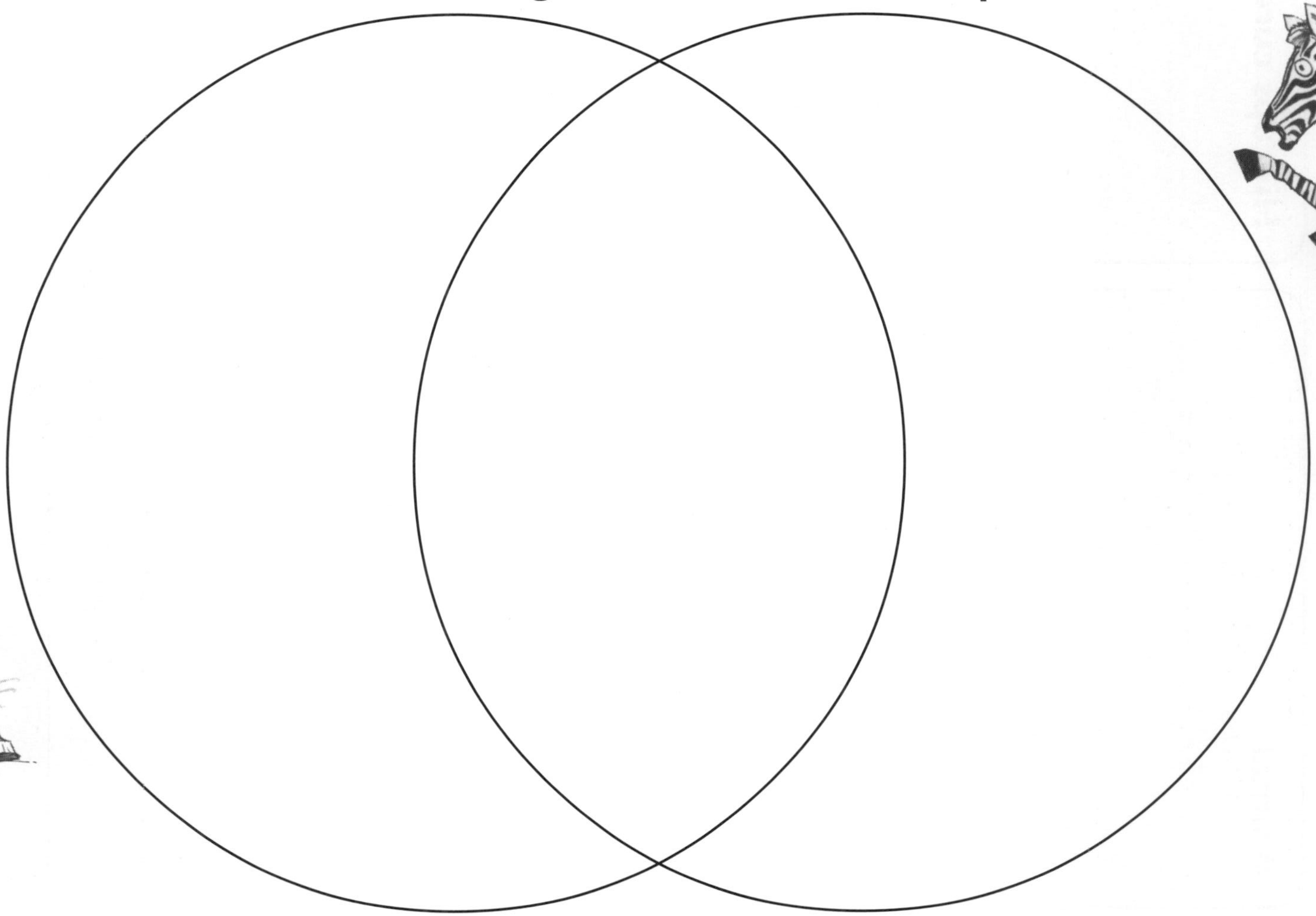

Name

Date

Mrs Zing or Dreamboat Zing?

"All that travelling has tired me out."

"Let's go home and have dinner."

"Nothing scares me!"

"It's like a roller-coaster ride!"

"There's only one cure for hiccups that I know of."

Dreamboat Zing

"An ugly monster!"

"Don't boast... and stop admiring yourself in the mirror."

"Shall I help you get dinner ready?"

"The Great White shark adores cheese and pickle sandwiches."

Mrs Zing

"But I'm so good-looking."

Name   Date

Make the story

to wake them up.

Then added, "Hic!"

"This cave is full of hungry vampire bats,"

and your hiccups will disappear."

"What are you doing?"

When you see their flapping wings,

explained Mrs Zing.

you'll be so scared, you'll go, 'Eeek!'

"I'm going to burst the balloon

asked Dreamboat Zing.

44

HE BABY WHO WOULDN'T GO TO BED

BY HELEN COOPER

About the book

This book describes the fantasy adventures of a very young child who is reluctant to go to bed. He escapes from his mother in a toy car and embarks upon an imaginary journey in which he meets a number of toy characters. All of these characters are, however, too tired to play with him. Eventually, as darkness envelops his fantasy world, his mother finds him and brings him back to his own bedroom. Here we see that the characters the Baby has met are really the toys from his bedroom, brought alive through his imagination. Helen Cooper's award-winning illustrations enrich the text by developing further layers of meaning, setting a background of the fading light of day, the glow of sunset and the gathering darkness.

The story is carefully presented with patterned language and interesting layout features, including changes in the size and distribution of print on the page. It explores the relationship between fantasy and reality, looking at familiar routines and conflicts between parents and children. The book takes the form of a flight of fantasy with a story structure and theme that is similar to Jill Murphy's *Whatever Next!*

Fantasy and reality

The idea of a journey from reality to fantasy is a common theme in stories for this age range. Like Maurice Sendak's *Where the Wild Things Are* (Red Fox) and Kit Wright's *Tigerella* (Scholastic), the story focuses on a child in the familiar setting of home who escapes from predictable, mundane events through the use of imagination. The inevitable resolution (bedtime) is postponed through a series of imaginary encounters. On the last double-page spread, in which the Mother is shown putting the Baby to bed, the two aspects of the book join together. The problem of the baby who wouldn't go to bed is solved within the story and at the same time, we appreciate that the fantasy objects are really the Baby's bedroom toys.

About the author

Helen Cooper has produced a number of high-quality children's picture books. *The Bear Under the Stairs* also explores the link between reality and fantasy – a bear visits the house of a boy called William and we are never quite sure if the bear is real or imagined. Similarly *Little Monster Did It!* involves the imaginary actions of a mischievous toy who takes the blame for real acts of jealousy.

Teaching opportunities

The baby who wouldn't go to bed is worth revisiting to explore its complexities. The fantasy element is driven by the dreamlike quality of the illustrations. The repetition and patterns in the text, with the *vrrruuum-chugga-chug* of the baby's car and the characters who all want to sleep, provide the language to evoke this mood. The symbolism of the marching soldiers who carry toothbrushes and the unwinding birds are more subtle clues that you can talk about with the children.

GUIDED READING NOTES

Introduce the book. Talk about the front cover. Draw attention to the title and the name of the author-illustrator. Do the children remember reading anything by Helen Cooper before? Explain, if necessary, that she writes the words and creates the pictures to go with them. Say that we can often learn a lot about a story before we begin reading it. Talk about how we can use the cover illustration to guess what the book might be about and also to think how it might appeal to us, or remind us of something else we have read or something we are interested in.

Re-read the title – *The baby who wouldn't go to bed*. What can the children predict about the story from this title? You might want to keep a note of

their suggestions. What can they see on the cover that helps this prediction? Is the small figure in the car the baby? Why doesn't he want to go to bed? Encourage the children to talk about their own experiences of bedtime. They may be able to talk about 'conflicts' between parents and babies at bedtime. What sort of things do babies (and young children) do to avoid going to bed? What do parents do in response?

Now read the whole of the book together. Ask the children to respond to this afterwards by describing their favourite part and telling you what they particularly liked about it. Turn back to look more closely at the incidents they remember well. Ask the children to recall the predictions they made in the introductory session. How accurate were they? If you kept a note of these from the first guided read, you can check back, but make sure the children understand that making predictions isn't simply about getting the 'right' answer. Predictions are

based on the information available up to that point and are our best guess about events to come in the story.

Talk about the main events in the story. It begins at bedtime in the familiar setting of the Baby's house, but he escapes from his mother and goes on a fantasy journey before he is found again, returns to the familiar setting and then goes to bed. Talk about the fantasy journey – do the children think that this really happened? Or was it a journey in the Baby's imagination? There is no right or wrong answer to the question – after all, the book itself is a story, a product of imagination – but use the discussion to introduce the terms *reality* and *fantasy*. Relate the idea of fantasy to the children's own role-play or playground play. The Baby in the story seems to like his little car with its ladder. Ask the children about their favourite toys and the imaginary play that they engage in with them.

Before reading the book again, review the events that get the story started. First, ask the children if they can remember how *The baby who wouldn't go to bed* begins, without looking at the book. How does the story start? Who is introduced on the first page and where are they? What is happening? Now turn to page 5 (taking the very first page in the book as page 1) and read it together. Suggest to the children that they could help you to read the dialogue with some expression. Divide up the group so that some of the children take on the voice of the Mother and some the voice of the Baby. Talk about how the characters might sound when they speak (for example, tired, cross; cheeky, pleading). Re-read page 5

together, trying to convey these feelings.

Summarise this work by establishing what the Baby wants to do and what the Mother wants the Baby to do. Look at the picture on page 5 and imagine what the characters are thinking, or what else they might say in addition to the text given. Ask the children what they would do next if they were Baby. *Why* doesn't he want to go to bed? What will Baby do next? Encourage the children to imagine how the Mother might be feeling. Would she feel tired, for instance? Discuss what the children would do next if they were Mother. Now ask the children if they can remember what does happen next. Check the children's awareness and understanding of the rest of the story.

Read from page 5 through to page 13. Stop here to look more closely at the picture. Ask the children to identify the passengers on the train. In order, we see the Three Little Pigs, the Frog Prince, Dick Whittington, the

Gingerbread Man, Humpty Dumpty, the Dish and the Spoon from 'Hey Diddle Diddle', Mother Goose and Little Red Riding Hood – other more shadowy and less familiar figures, including a giraffe, are shown on the other side of the tunnel. Look at their faces and establish what all these characters are doing. Why has Helen Cooper shown them all asleep? Talk about what else the picture shows. Look at the train's expression and where it is going. Read the signs that show the station and the depot and discuss how these relate to the text of the story. Re-read what the Baby says – *'Race you to the <u>station</u> for a jolly good smash-up'* – and what the train says in reply – *'I'm going home to my <u>depot</u>, and so should you.'* (You may need to explain the word *depot* to the children.) Now examine the picture to find out why the train couldn't get to the station even if it wanted to.

CONT. . .

CONT. . .

To conclude this session, talk about the colours that Helen Cooper has used in her illustration across this double-page spread. What does the colour of the sky suggest about the sun and daylight? Recall how on page 5 the Baby said that he didn't want to go to sleep because *It's still light*. Look through the book to see how daylight slowly turns to sunset and darkness as the Baby's journey goes on. Ask the children to remember how this happens as they read on through the story.

Read on to the bottom of page 21 – *Someone who was looking for the Baby...* Discuss the illustration on this double page with the children. Ask them what the source of the light on the path in the top right-hand corner is. Who might be looking for the Baby? Look carefully at the picture and ask the children to think about the mood or feelings that it conveys. Pay particular attention to the use of dark, cool colours, the shadows, the sleeping birds and other animals and the viewpoint of looking down from a distance on the Baby who is a very small, isolated figure behind his stationary car. Talk about the stillness of the scene and point out the wind-up birds. They have all wound down and stopped moving, like the Baby. Re-read the text on page 20, asking the children to spot where the language in the description fits this scene. Make notes on this on the flip chart, for example *he'd gone as far as he could*; *he stood quite still, all alone*; *the sleeping world* surrounds him.

Read to the end of the book.
Show the children how the Baby is now safely back in the familiar setting of his house and the tension at the beginning has been resolved. The baby's fantasy journey is over. Ask the children to imagine what the characters' feelings are now. Again, tell them to think about what the Mother might do next. Encourage them to justify their opinions with reference to the book. It's unlikely that the Mother is going to go out or watch television – after all she is in her pyjamas and the text describes her as being *ever so weary*, but not able to go to bed until Baby does (page 24).

Turn to pages 30–1. Talk about the picture and draw the children's attention to the toys around the room. Look for the characters from the Baby's fantasy journey. Can the children remember some of his encounters and conversations with them? For example, the Baby wants to roar with the tiger, but the tiger says *'Night time is for snoring not roaring.'* Use this picture to retell the story together from memory.

ACTIVITY NOTES

Bedtime

Objective: to explore relationships between characters and understand how characters change.

Resources: photocopiable page 53, writing materials.

Activity: Show the children the shortened 'cartoon' version of the beginning and ending of the story given on the photocopiable sheet. Discuss as a group what might be put into the speech bubbles. You could use the words at the bottom of the sheet as prompts or, for more flexibility, encourage the children to think of their own words and phrases. Demonstrate that in the first frame the Mother and the Baby are not getting on very well and the other two frames (after the fantasy journey) show that their loving relationship is restored. Ask the children to complete the speech bubbles on the sheet, working individually or in pairs.

Fantasy journey

Objective: to sequence events in the story.

Resources: photocopiable page 54, copies of *The baby who wouldn't go to bed*, scissors, glue, paper.

Activity: Introduce this activity by asking the children to recall the sequence of events in the Baby's fantasy journey in his little car. Browse through the book together whilst you are doing this. Then ask the children to work independently, cutting out the character pictures from the sheet and sticking them onto paper in the order in which the Baby met them. Advise the children to make sure they are happy with their sequence before they stick the pictures down. For less able children, you could copy the pictures onto card and cut them out, and use the individual cards to sequence and retell the story.

Where have you been?

Objectives: to recognise characters; to develop recognition of core vocabulary used in the story.

Resources: photocopiable page 55, writing materials.

Activity: This activity, using an illustration from towards the end of *The baby who wouldn't go to bed*, encourages further recall of the fantasy journey, asking the children to identify and name the objects (that become characters) in the Baby's bedroom. Together, read through the core words given on the sheet, and ask the children if they remember these characters. Explain that you want them to draw a line to join the word with the corresponding object shown in the picture.

Extension: Develop this activity further by encouraging children to find characters and objects in the picture that are not mentioned in the written text of the story (for example, the wind-up bird, the squirrel, the fairy-tale books). Discuss where each of these would be included on a timeline of the journey.

SCHOLASTIC LITERACY CENTRES

And so to bed

Objectives: to recall fantasy locations from the story; to explore story events by playing a board game.

Resources: photocopiable page 56 copied onto card, counters, dice.

Activity: Explain to the children how to play the game, using their counters and dice to recreate events from the Baby's fantasy that he encounters on his way to bed. Playing in pairs, they should take it in turns to roll the dice and move their counter along the board according to their score. Before letting the children start their games, talk about the idea of winning this particular game. Would the Baby prefer to take the journey *quickly* or *slowly*? Does he want to get to bed sooner or later? Explain that if they take him to the castle, for example, instead of turning off towards the bridge, they will need to come back to rejoin the route the Baby actually took. The children may decide that in this game the winner is the last person into bed!

Talking toys

Objective: to identify dialogue and match it with characters.

Resources: photocopiable page 57, copies of *The baby who wouldn't go to bed*, writing materials.

Activity: Introduce this activity by reading through and discussing the dialogue in the speech bubbles on the photocopiable sheet. Can the children remember who said what? Advise them to choose from the characters given at the bottom of the sheet. (There are more characters than they will need.) Some of the children may need to refer to the book before completing the sheet on their own, but encourage those who can to attempt it from memory.

More on the way

Objective: to develop additional characters for the fantasy and imagine what these characters might say.

Resources: photocopiable page 58, copies of *The baby who wouldn't go to bed*, writing materials.

Activity: Remind the children of some of the patterned language in *The baby who wouldn't go to bed*: *Night time is for snoring, not roaring; Night time is for dreaming, not parading* and so on. Now show the children the photocopiable sheet on which they need to make up their own sentences based on this pattern. Draw attention to the new toy characters illustrated. Ask the children to imagine that the Baby also met these figures on his journey and to think about what they would say. Go through an example together before asking the children to complete the sheet. For instance, next to the tricycle, you might put *Night time is for resting, not racing*.

Extension: Children could think of more objects or toys of their own. These simple sentences could be joined together to make a class poem and this could be revisited in subsequent shared reading sessions.

One more time

Objectives: to use the story structure to develop creative ideas; to create further fantasy encounters for the Baby.

Resources: photocopiable page 59, writing and drawing materials.

Activity: Ask the children to look at the illustrations given on the photocopiable sheet and to think of further toy characters of their own to add, then think about using all of these to plan another sleepy fantasy journey for the Baby. Draw attention to the way the journey can be subdivided into three stages – it has a beginning, a middle and an ending. Share the children's ideas before they start working on the sheet themselves. Explain that they should use pictures and words to plan their sequence of events in the style of *The baby who wouldn't go to bed*. These can then be used to support an oral telling of their story.

Extension: Children could write and illustrate their own story or make a book: *The baby who wouldn't go to bed again*.

Night time

Objective: to develop understanding of pattern in the dialogue.

Resources: photocopiable page 60, completed photocopiable page 58, copies of *The baby who wouldn't go to bed*, scissors, glue, paper.

Activity: Remind the children that each time the Baby asks one of the toy characters *Let's play* or *march* or *have a party*, the character replies with a sentence that begins *Night time is for...* You can refer to the work done on 'More on the way' on photocopiable page 58 to draw attention to this. Ask the children to read the text on the sheet, then cut out the strips and match up each request of Baby's with the answer he gets. Advise the children to look in the book to check before they stick the strips onto a sheet of paper.

Act it out

Objective: to develop a sense of setting through role-play of the Baby's journey.

Resources: photocopiable page 61, coloured writing materials, scissors, large sheet of grey or black sugar paper, small toy car.

Activity: This is a collaborative group activity to involve children in role-play based on *The baby who wouldn't go to bed*. Use the picture cards on the sheet for indications of settings. Help the children to cut them out, colour them in and paste them onto the sugar paper to make a winding road or path. It may help to draw an outline road on the sugar paper for the children before you start. The children could make their props stand up by folding the cards along the line and sticking the bottom section to the sugar paper. Then ask them to retell the story through role-play, concentrating particularly on the dialogue, as they push the small toy car along the road. Ask the children to work within the group to decide on which roles to take.

Dream, dream, dream...

Objective: to describe the actions of characters in the fantasy story.

Resources: photocopiable page 62, completed photocopiable page 55, copies of *The baby who wouldn't go to bed*, writing materials.

Activity: Talk about what the children can see in the bedroom picture on page 31 of *The baby who wouldn't go to bed* and remind them of the work they did for 'Where have you been?' on photocopiable page 55. Now ask them to think about what the toy characters were doing or where they were when the Baby met them on his fantasy journey. Tell them to go through the book, looking for words that describe action, and examining the pictures, and also to consider what the Baby had really been doing all this time. Ask them to write a brief description for each character on the photocopiable sheet, for example *The soldiers were going back to their castle*, then share what they have written in a plenary session.

Mother and Baby are doing fine

Objective: to explore the story from different perspectives.

Resources: flip chart or board.

Activity: Within the dream/fantasy context of the story, encourage the children to consider how the Mother might have felt at the beginning of the story, how she felt when the Baby 'went off' and then when she 'found' him and put him to bed. Ask the children to suggest words you could use to describe each stage and make a note of these in three columns on the flip chart. Perhaps the Mother felt *fed up* or *angry* at the start of the story; she may have been *sad*, *tired* or even *lonely* or *worried* when the Baby went off; and *happy* or *relieved* in finally putting him to bed. Follow this with a discussion about how the Baby felt at each stage during the story, for example *cheeky, energetic* or *naughty* in the beginning; *sleepy* or *scared* later; and *tired* or *happy* at the end.

Message from Baby

Objectives: to imagine what the Baby might say or feel during the fantasy adventure; to write in role.

Resources: photocopiable page 63, writing materials.

Activity: Encourage the children to reflect on the events of the story specifically from the Baby's point of view. Explain that the photocopiable sheet shows Baby somewhere in the middle of his journey and that the thought bubble represents him imagining what he might write to the Mother – so it is laid out like a letter. Work on the sheet initially as a shared composition and encourage the children to describe events and actions rather than simply listing the toy characters encountered. Ask them to think about how they would tell their story in a letter to a relative, if *they* were on a long journey.

Name

Date

Bedtime

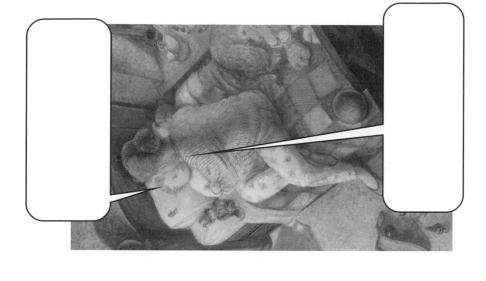

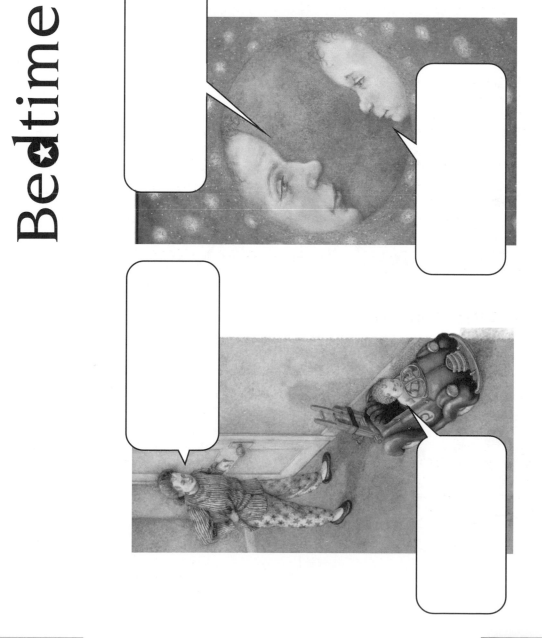

Bedtime

Y-a-w-n

Alright then

No

SCHOLASTIC LITERACY CENTRES

Name

Date

Fantasy journey

birds

tiger

musicians

moon

train

soldiers

Name

Date

Where have you been?

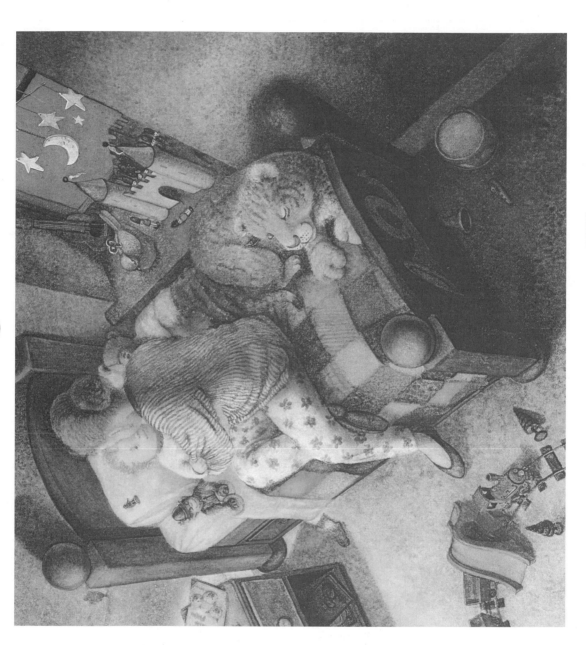

tiger

soldiers

musicians

moon

train

castle

Name

Date

And so to bed

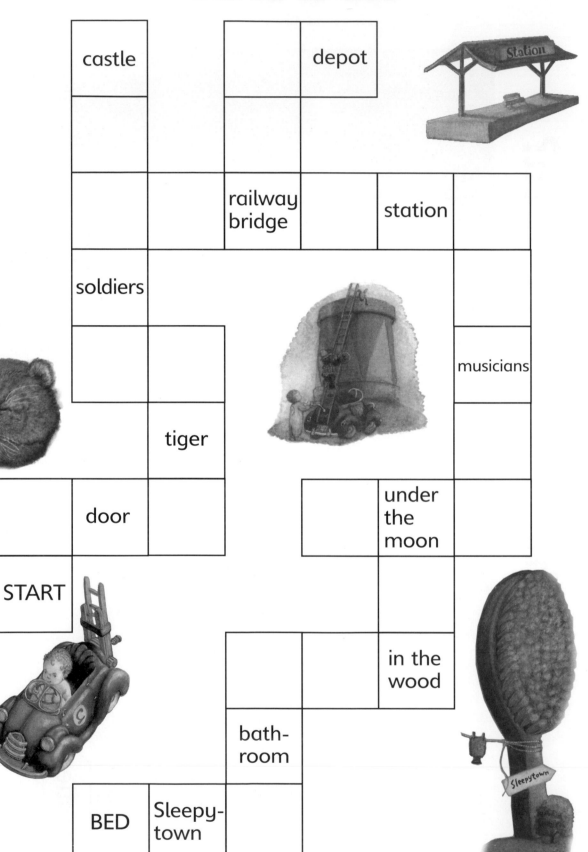

castle

depot

railway bridge

station

soldiers

musicians

tiger

door

under the moon

START

in the wood

bath-room

BED | Sleepy-town

Name   Date

Talking toys

Give us a lift home, and we'll play you a lullaby.

_____

We're going back to our castle.

_____

I'm going to stay up all night.

_____

I'm going home to my depot.

_____

musicians	soldiers	Mother
birds	train	Baby	moon

Name _____ Date _____

More on the way

Night time is for _____

not _____.

Night time is for _____

not _____.

Night time is for _____

not _____.

Night time is for _____

not _____.

fiction **yellow**

Fantasy worlds

Name

Date

One more time

Name   Date

Night time

Let's play at roaring.	Night time is for dreaming.
Let's march.	Night time is for resting.
Let's have a party.	Night time is for snoring.
Can't we have a midnight feast?	We're really, really tired.
Race you to the station.	It's bedtime.

fiction **yellow**

Fantasy worlds

Name _____   Date _____

Act it out

fold

fold

fold

Name _____   Date _____

Dream, dream, dream...

SCHOLASTIC LITERACY CENTRES

SCHOLASTIC

fiction **yellow**

Fantasy worlds

Name _____ Date _____

Message from Baby

Dear Mother,

I

Fantasy Island

Background

This advertisement aims to encourage children to visit a (fictitious) holiday location. It draws on their experience of fantasy in *The baby who wouldn't go to bed* and builds on it by introducing another familiar type of text. This example introduces key features of persuasive writing, including an eye-catching design, a title that rouses interest and a list of exciting attractions. The advert concludes with contact details. Introduce the children to the particular language features of persuasive texts and the importance of layout. Remember to emphasise that the aim of this text is to get the reader to go to Fantasy Island (rather than somewhere else). You can relate this piece to a collection of other persuasive leaflets, posters, printed adverts and so on. A useful starting point is to make a scrapbook of flyers that advertise local attractions.

■ Draw the children's attention to the layout of the text on photocopiable page 66. Talk about the title and the illustrations. Is this eye-catching? Does it make them want to go there? Now read through the advertisement together. Ask the children what would make them want to go to Fantasy Island and why they find the attractions interesting. If they don't think that they are particularly interesting, ask them to suggest alternatives and consider changes to the leaflet.

■ Encourage the children to think about the tone of the advertisement and discuss who produces publicity for attractions like this. You may need to explain that they are normally written by marketing experts who present the material for the owners. Ask the children if they think that the advertisement has a friendly tone to it. How is this achieved? Demonstrate that there are several strategies at work here. First, the leaflet uses the pronouns *you* and *us* which suggest a familiar and informal relationship. Second, it encourages the reader by stating that a visit would be the experience of a lifetime and would make *dreams come true*. Third, it makes arrangements sound easy for potential visitors – they only need to book now (they pay later!) and they can phone or visit the website.

■ Ask the children to use photocopiable page 67 to plan an imaginary journey to Fantasy Island. Draw attention to the journey structure in *The baby who wouldn't go to bed*. Encourage the children to make notes about the journey there, events that happen on the island and the return journey.

■ Photocopiable page 68 prompts the children to think in more detail about what visitors might be able to do and see, and what might happen on the island. Encourage them to select from the suggestions given (crossing out any they don't want to include) and to add ideas of their own in similar note form.

■ As part of their imaginary visit to Fantasy Island, the children can use their ideas from photocopiable page 68 and the prompts on photocopiable page 69 to write a letter to their friends describing their adventures. In preparing for this activity, encourage the children to make comparisons with *The baby who wouldn't go to bed*, for instance the toys that 'come to life' and the friendly monsters who could fall asleep.

■ Develop a role-play based on an enquiry from a party who have read the advert. Tell the children to imagine they are members of this group. Advise them to think about why they want to go, how old the people in the group are and how much spending money they have. Practise a role-play in which one of the children makes a phone call to Fantasy Island. Make sure the child has a number of questions to ask based on the needs of the party. For example, *Will it be suitable for a six year old? Will there be baby-changing facilities? Are there reductions for larger family groups? When does it open?* When you try the role-play for the first time, pick a confident child and take the part of the owner of Fantasy Island yourself. After this, the children can work in pairs to experiment with their own role-plays.

■ Suggest that further publicity may be needed to promote Fantasy Island. Explain to the children that they are going to plan a short television commercial aimed at the younger visitor. Make a list of the children's ideas about what should be in the commercial. They could then work in small groups to design visual effects, create a storyboard, design a layout on the computer and write and rehearse commentaries or sound effects that will be used. Bring these ideas together in a plenary session and ask a couple of the groups to act out their commercials.

assessment

ASSESSMENT NOTES

True or false?

Assessment focus: to recall events in *The baby who wouldn't go to bed*; to distinguish between events that are in the story and those that are not.
Resources: photocopiable page 70, writing materials.
Activity: Read through the sheet with the children and explain that they should decide whether each statement given is true or false. Complete the first statement as an example, circling *true* or *false*. The children need to remember the story in some detail and think about all the events that happened.

Fact or fantasy?

Assessment focus: to demonstrate understanding of the difference between fact and fantasy.
Resources: photocopiable page 71, writing materials.
Activity: Ask the children if they can tell you what the word *fantasy* means. By now they should at least be able to relate the idea of a fantasy story to their own imaginative play. They may use the words *pretend* and *real*, for instance, when distinguishing the two. Remind the children of the fantastical things that occur in *The baby who wouldn't go to bed*. Introduce the photocopiable sheet and demonstrate the procedure of ticking a statement if it is true in real life, and a cross if it is 'pretend' or fantasy – so the first statement gets a cross!

Fantasy Island

Be happy!
It's the chance
of a lifetime.

Visit us at
Fantasy Island
and make
your dreams
come true.

*We promise you'll never look
back. Your visit will include:*

friendly
monsters

talking
animals

exciting toys that
come to life

delicious meals
(eat as much as
you like)

and FUN all day long.

Contact us on 0282 975747 to book or visit
our website www.fantasyisland.net

Book now and pay later.

Name _____   Date _____

OFF YOU GO!

Fantasy Island

What happens there?
What do you see?

SCHOLASTIC LITERACY CENTRES

How do you get there?
What do you pass on
the way?

How do you get back?

Your home

Name

Date

On the island

toy cars that you can drive

friendly monsters

talking bears

robots you can control

birds that can fly you around the island

giraffes you can ride

a lake of ice cream

Name _____   Date _____

From the island

Fantasy Island
No day at all

| Who are you writing to? | Dear _____ |

How was the journey to get here?

_____

_____

_____

What have you been doing?

_____

_____

What have you seen?

_____

_____

Are you enjoying yourself?

_____

_____

_____

_____

Name   Date

True or false?

The Baby had a toy tiger on his bed.	true false
The musicians played a lullaby.	true false
The train went to the station.	true false
The Baby didn't want to go to bed at the beginning.	true false
The Baby stayed up all night.	true false
The soldiers were carrying drums.	true false
The moon dozed off.	true false
The Mother couldn't find the Baby.	true false

Name _____ Date _____

Fact or fantasy?

✔ or ✗

Babies drive their toy cars out of the house when they don't want to go to bed.	
When it's still light, some babies think it's too early for bed.	
Babies have toys in their bedrooms.	
You can climb up to the moon on a ladder.	
Toy trains can talk to you.	
You might yawn when you're very tired.	
A lullaby can send you to sleep.	

SCHOLASTIC LITERACY CENTRES

fiction yellow
Fantasy worlds

WHATEVER NEXT!

BY JILL MURPHY

About the book

This is another story of the Baby Bear character from *Peace at Last* and describes his fantastic journey to the moon and back before bathtime. It features a classic fantasy element, with a structure and theme that is very similar to *The baby who wouldn't go to bed*. Although the central character is a bear, children will recognise the idea of an extended fantasy through their own imaginary play. The make-believe adventure, meeting new friends and taking provisions for the journey is a common theme that Jill Murphy builds on by creating a visit to the moon. The story includes everyday objects (such as the cardboard box and Baby Bear's own teddy) that contrast reality with fantasy. Jill Murphy's narrative closely follows Baby Bear's journey, but the story is based in a familiar domestic context, finishing with Mrs Bear's amusement and disbelief as she says to Baby Bear *'You and your stories. Whatever next?'*

A story within a story

Like many popular children's stories, there are actually two stories in *Whatever Next!*. The first story approximates to real life as the parent prepares an evening bath before putting the child to bed. The child – as is often the case – has other ideas, and this is the second and central story: Baby Bear's journey to the moon and back.

About the author

Jill Murphy has developed a distinctive style of combining illustration and text in her picture books. Her interest in writing and illustration began in childhood. She wrote *The Worst Witch* (Puffin Books) when she was 17 and when it was published several years later, it quickly became a best-seller. Jill Murphy trained at art school and had a variety of jobs before becoming a professional writer and illustrator at the age of 27. *Peace at Last*, the first story to feature Baby Bear, earned a commendation in the Kate Greenaway awards. Her books show the humorous side of the often demanding relationships between parents and children. She explores everyday situations using animals such as bears (as in *Peace at Last* and *Whatever Next!*) or elephants (*A Quiet Night In* and *Five Minutes' Peace*) as the main characters and her illustrations show domestic life with its familiar objects and routines. Simple gestures and subtle facial expressions are used to convey the characters' feelings. These features help to draw the children into the text and enrich the meanings provided by the words.

Teaching opportunities

Children enjoy the simple narrative structure of *Whatever Next!* and quickly identify with the domestic routines and the idea of an outing that includes a picnic. The fantasy element of this book takes the form of a journey (making clear parallels with *The baby who wouldn't go to bed* and *Where the Wild Things Are*) and this provides a good opportunity for discussing the children's experiences of outings and holidays.

GUIDED READING NOTES

Introduce Whatever Next! by discussing the front cover and then the title page. Ask the children to read the title and author-illustrator. Do the children recognise Jill Murphy's name? Explain that she writes the text and draws the illustrations as well. Find out what the children know about picture book authors and use the notes on the previous page to provide some background information about Jill Murphy. Now look at the endpapers of the book. This illustration is a double-page spread that contains an extended version of the front cover picture, showing more rooftops and the owl, who comes to have a significant part in the story. Ask the children to name the objects and animals it shows. Discuss this picture in more detail and use it to encourage speculation about the story. Ask the children to think about what kind of story it is going to be. Is it a factual book or a story? How do they know? Go on to ask if they think the story will contain real or fantasy characters and events (or both). What clues do they have? Emphasise the similarity between fantasy in a story and their own role-playing in which they act as if they are a character involved in real events.

Now look at the title page and encourage the children to develop their thoughts on what the book is about. What other characters might appear? Who might the bear be looking up to? How has he got so grubby? Make notes of the children's predictions to return to later.

Read the first two pages (pages 7–8, taking 1 as the very first page in the book). Check the children's understanding of the story so far. Who are the two characters? What does Baby Bear want to do and what does Mrs Bear want? Look at the picture on page 9 and ask the children to imagine what the bears are thinking. If the illustration had thought bubbles, what might be written in them? Ask the children what they would do next if they were Baby Bear. Encourage them to relate this to their own experiences. Are there times in the day when they would rather be doing something else? You might want to talk about getting ready for school, for example, as well as going to bed or having a bath. What do the children think Baby Bear is going to do next, and why? How might Mrs Bear react? Do they think Baby Bear will be able to find a rocket? At this point, the children could refer to the cover and endpaper illustrations they looked at in the previous session. Could Baby Bear really fly to the moon in a cardboard box?

Read the rest of the story (pages 10–36). See if the children's predictions were right, but stress that making a prediction isn't simply about correctly guessing what

CONT. . .

74

happens. Talk about the main event in the story. *Whatever Next!* begins in Baby Bear's house, but he has an adventure before he has his bath and goes to bed. What is that adventure? Did Baby Bear *really* go to the moon? Introduce the terms *reality* and *fantasy* and, if appropriate, compare this book with *Dreamboat Zing*. The children might appreciate that there are two levels of fantasy here. Bears don't talk, wear clothes and live in houses – in fact they *can* be quite dangerous animals! Nevertheless, bears are very popular in children's stories, from the traditional story of Goldilocks and the Three Bears to the picture book classic *Teddy Bear Coalman* by Phoebe and Selby Worthington to

contemporary stories like Helen Cooper's *The Bear Under the Stairs*. So, the first level of fantasy involves accepting that 'in the story' (as in many other animal stories), Baby Bear and Mrs Bear behave like human beings, as their names suggest. A second level of fantasy concerns Baby Bear's journey to the moon. Did he *really* go to the moon? Can we accept that within the context of the story he did, or was it purely an imaginary journey? Discuss this idea with the children. There is no right or wrong answer – the presentation is ambiguous and interpretation depends on the reader.

Before looking again at the conversation at the picnic and just after (pages 24–7), ask the children if they can remember what Baby Bear did on the moon. Can they remember who was there and what they had for their picnic? What was Baby Bear's reason for coming back home? Now look at the illustration on page 25 to check how well the children recall details of the picnic. Re-read pages

24–7, telling the children to look out for the reason Baby Bear gives for why it's time to go home. On page 24, he complains that *There's nobody here* and *It's a bit boring*, but his main reason is that he remembers about bathtime. Ask the children to find where he mentions this. (On page 26.)

Focus on the last four pages (pages 31–5). Begin by studying the illustration on page 31 and ask the children where Baby Bear has just come from. *Look at his face. How do you think he feels? Why is he so dirty?* Point out the food left over from the picnic. What can the children tell you about it? Why is it half eaten?

Now read to the end of the story. Ask the children to imagine what Mrs Bear thought of Baby Bear's story. Did she believe him? How did she feel when she saw that he was so dirty? How did he get so dirty? Discuss what she means when she says *'Whatever next?'* and explain that the expression is often used to convey disbelief.

Remind the children that the story is called *Whatever Next!*. Read the first part of the blurb on the back cover to reinforce this – *The moon and back before bathtime? Whatever next!* Consider again whether or not Mrs Bear believes Baby Bear's explanation. Perhaps she thinks the adventure is a fantasy of his imagination.

Re-read the whole story and use this read-through to demonstrate reading with expression. Ask the children to join in with you when you are reading what Baby Bear says (on pages 7, 18, 24, 26 and 34). It's a good idea to rehearse some of this first.

Encourage the children to put suitable expression into their voices at each stage. Perhaps he says *'Can I go to the moon?'* with mischief in his voice; *'There's nobody here'* and *'It's a bit boring'* may be said in more subdued tones, and so on. Ask the children to help you to decide on an appropriate tone for Mrs Bear. Perhaps she would sound a little cross when she says *'No you can't. It's bathtime.'* Ask the children how they think Mrs Bear feels at the end of the story. Look at the illustration as well as her words given in the text. (For example, she has *finally* managed to lure Baby Bear into the bath and she can soon put him to bed; she is amused by what he says.) How could these feelings be conveyed when she speaks? Draw attention to the line on page 34, after Baby Bear has retold his adventure, in which Jill Murphy writes *Mrs Bear laughed*. Use this as a clue as to how to read the concluding dialogue. Now re-read the whole story together, trying to make it sound as entertaining as possible.

Focus on pages 12–13 to discuss the roles played by the verbal and visual elements of the book. Talk about the illustration on page 13 first and ask the children to describe what it shows. Encourage them to use factual language in their descriptions, such as *Baby Bear is sitting on a mat by a blue door. He is pulling on yellow rubber boots.* You could note these 'factual' descriptions in one column on a flip chart or board. Now read the sentence on page 12. What additional information does it provide and how does it work with the line drawing above it? The illustrations show Baby Bear collecting various familiar objects from around the house, whereas the text refers to items such as the *space-helmet* and *space-boots* that are important in his fantasy journey.

You could summarise these discussions by adding to the column on the flip chart, heading it *What the pictures tell us*. For example, *The bear is looking for things to play with*. In a second column, headed *What the writing tells us*, put contrasting notes, such as *He finds a space-helmet and space-boots*.

ACTIVITY NOTES

Can I go to the moon?

Objectives: to recall elements and objects in the story; to practise the vocabulary introduced in the story.

Resources: photocopiable page 81 copied onto card and laminated if possible, spare sets of objects from photocopiable page 81, counters and dice.

Activity: See if the children can remember what Baby Bear takes with him on his journey to the moon. Read through the labels on the photocopiable sheet together, then organise the children into pairs and explain how to play the game. They take it in turns to move along the board by throwing the dice. If a player lands on a shaded square, he or she collects one of the objects needed to get to the moon – food, space-boots, space-helmet and rocket. (If an object is picked up by one player, it does not prevent the other player picking up the same object from another set.) The winner is the first player to reach the moon with all four objects.

Is it real?

Objective: to consider reality and fantasy in the story.

Resources: copies of *Whatever Next!*, flip chart or board.

Activity: Draw two columns on the flip chart. Talk about imagined events and reality and help the children to distinguish between the two. Explain how *Whatever Next!* is a fantasy story, but that a fantasy always contains recognisable objects and some everyday events. Label one of the columns on the flip chart *fantasy* and the other *reality*. Ask the children to help you make a list of items and events from the story for each column. For example, you might have *window, curtains, mop, apple, moon, cat* and *dressing gown* in the reality column. In the fantasy column, you might have *bears and owls that talk*, *flying to the moon in a box*, *colander space-helmet*. Keep the lists, if possible, for use in a later activity.

Is it a bird?

Objectives: to imagine thoughts and feelings in a fantasy setting; to think about events from different points of view.

Resources: photocopiable page 82, copies of *Whatever Next!*, writing materials.

Activity: Ask the children to study the illustration on page 21 of the story, where Baby Bear and the owl pass the aeroplane. Discuss what is going on with the children. The plane is flown by bear pilots; some of the passengers look as though they are waving, and the text confirms this. What does Baby Bear think when he sees the plane? What do the crew and passengers think when they see a bear and an owl in a cardboard box? Contrast the way these fantasy events are presented with how they would appear in real life. Ask the children how they think a pilot and aeroplane passengers would *really* react if they saw in the sky a bear wearing a colander, with an owl, both in a cardboard box! *If you were near a large aeroplane that came <u>roaring</u> out of the clouds, how would you feel?* (Probably frightened.) In the fantasy context of the story, however, this all adds to the excitement and Baby Bear simply waves. Show the children the photocopiable sheet and go through one of the character's thoughts as a model. Then encourage the children to work independently.

A visit to the moon

Objectives: to recognise and label characters and objects from the story; to practise key vocabulary.
Resources: photocopiable page 83, scissors, glue.
Activity: Read the labels at the bottom of the photocopiable sheet with the children and see if they remember the objects and characters from the story. Explain to the children they should cut out the labels and paste them in the correct places around the illustration.

Who said that?

Objective: to match dialogue from the story to the correct character.
Resources: photocopiable page 84, copies of *Whatever Next!*, writing materials.
Activity: This activity requires children to match the speech to the appropriate character – either Mrs Bear or the owl. See if the children can do this orally, from memory, but let them look at a copy of the book if necessary. This activity can be done in pairs to encourage collaboration and discussion. Ask the children to complete the photocopiable sheet by drawing a line to connect each speech bubble with the illustration of the appropriate character.

The moon and back

Objectives: to develop understanding of the story structure; to recall events; to retell parts of the story from the main character's point of view.
Resources: photocopiable page 85, writing materials.
Activity: Look at the illustration on the photocopiable sheet and show the children where it occurs in the book – right at the end of the story. Ask the children to imagine that after his adventure and his warm bath, Baby Bear goes to sleep and dreams about his visit to the moon. Can the children remember what happened first? Where did Baby Bear want to go? How did he get himself ready to go to the moon? What did he need to gather together? Scribe a brief answer in the first thought bubble. If the children suggest that you start by writing *Baby Bear wanted...* remind them that they are imagining they are Baby Bear and having his thoughts and dreams, so they will be writing in the first person – *I wanted...* Go on to ask the children to recall what happened on the way and then what Baby Bear and the owl did once they landed on the moon. Lastly, discuss what could be put in the fourth thought bubble about the journey home. Then ask the children to complete the sheet for themselves.

More than a box

Objectives: to explore the role of imagination in the story; to look at alternative ways to develop a fantasy world.
Resources: photocopiable page 86, writing materials, cardboard boxes. For the extension – craft materials and equipment.

Activity: Prepare for this activity by making a small collection of cardboard boxes of different shapes. Explain how in fantasy, as in play, we use our imaginations in letting objects represent (or stand for) something else. Ask the children how Baby Bear uses his imagination in *Whatever Next!*. Show them the picture of Baby Bear on page 11. Point out that he has found a box, but to him it is a rocket. Go through your collection of boxes, asking the children what the different boxes could be. For example, a circular cheese box could be a wheel or a fairground roundabout, a cereal box could be a truck or a bed. Once the children have grasped the idea, ask them to use the photocopiable sheet to record their own ideas in words and pictures.

Extension: This activity could be developed through box-modelling. Help the children to make box-model rockets for three-dimensional representation of events in the story. They could also be encouraged to use other media, such as large construction apparatus.

Questions, questions

Objectives: to recall events in the story; to read question words beginning *wh* and provide meaningful responses.

Resources: photocopiable page 87, scissors, glue, paper.

Activity: Explain to the children that all the questions on the left-hand side of the photocopiable sheet are based on the story *Whatever Next!* and that the answers are provided on the right, but not in the correct order. Model reading the questions and answers, re-reading and then working out the answer for each question. 'Think out loud' so the children can follow the process. Ask the children to cut out the panel of questions and paste it onto a separate sheet of paper. Then they can cut out the answers and match them to the questions one by one.

Could you?

Objectives: to develop understanding of fantasy and reality; to respond to the factual accuracy of statements.

Resources: photocopiable page 88, writing materials, flip chart or board.

Activity: Explain that some things in *Whatever Next!* are based very much in everyday life – reality. Other elements of the story are unlikely or impossible and purely imaginative – fantasy. Remind the children of the activity 'Is it real?' on page 76 and display the lists again. Draw the children's attention to the first example on this photocopiable sheet. Notice how *No* is crossed out and ask the children why they think this is? (They should be able to tell you that yes, you *could* have a bath before you go to bed.) Read the second example together and work out whether the answer to that question would be *Yes* or *No* – is it possible in real life or only something that could happen in a fantasy? Ask the children to explain what they will cross out and why. Now ask them to complete the rest of the activity, working individually or in pairs. Advise the children to read the questions carefully, looking out for the details. For example, it is possible to fly to the moon, but not in a cardboard box.

Extension: Ask children to design a similar list that combines fact and fantasy statements (not necessarily based on *Whatever Next!*). They can then work with a partner to test them out.

Getting ready

Objectives: to sequence events in the story; to match captions with illustrations.
Resources: photocopiable page 89, copies of *Whatever Next!*, scissors, glue, paper.
Activity: Ask the children to cut out the pictures and captions from the photocopiable sheet, and explain that they will be sticking them onto the blank paper. Can the children remember the sequence of events in the story and tell you which of the pictures comes first? Do they recall which part of the story all the pictures come from? Let them refer to the book if they need to. Now ask them to read the sentences about events in the story and look for the right caption to go with one of the pictures. Once the children have the hang of the activity, ask them to pair up the illustrations with the captions and stick them down together on the sheet of paper. Remind the children that the pairs should be in the correct order to retell that particular part of the story.

WHOOSH!

Objectives: to use sentences from the story to encourage reading for meaning; to practise positional vocabulary.
Resources: photocopiable page 90, writing materials, toy bear and small cardboard box (optional).
Activity: Begin by reading with the children the positional words from the chimney on the photocopiable sheet. Ask the children what all the words have in common. (They all indicate *where* things happen.) If this is a difficult concept for some of the children, demonstrate with the toy bear and cardboard box, standing him *by* or *next to* the box, *on* the box and so on. Now read through the sentences on the sheet, pausing to emphasise where words are missing. Explain that there may be more than one word that makes sense in the space in a particular sentence, for example *The rain dripped on/through Baby Bear's helmet*. By process of elimination, the children should be able to identify the positional word used in Jill Murphy's text. You might want to go all the way through the sheet with the children, working out each word in turn, but without recording the answers, before asking the children to complete it independently.
Extension: Children could identify and collect prepositions in their wider reading or from other popular picture books, such as *Each Peach Pear Plum* by Janet and Allan Ahlberg (Viking) or Eric Hill's *Where's Spot* (Frederick Warne).

Look at the state of you!

Objectives: to identify with another character's perspective; to justify responses to the text.
Resources: copies of *Whatever Next!*. For the extension – art and craft materials, long strips of paper, writing materials.
Activity: Mrs Bear doesn't know that Baby Bear has been to the moon. She just sees a grubby bear in rubber boots, clutching a colander. Explain this to the children then look together at the picture on page 33. Talk about the objects shown. What might Mrs Bear think that Baby Bear has been doing? (Playing? Being naughty?) Does she

believe Baby Bear when he says *'I found a rocket and went to visit the moon'*? Encourage the children to give reasons for their answers: *I don't think she believes him because...*

Extension: Use this discussion activity to create a wall display. Ask a small group of children to make a large collage picture based on page 33. Use strips of paper to record the sentences based on the structure above (for example, *I think she believes him because he's covered in soot*) and place these around the collage. Give the display a title like 'Would *you* believe him?'

The long journey

Objectives: to look at how language is used to suggest the passage of time; to see the effect of repeated language.

Resources: flip chart or board. For the extension – fantasy story books.

Activity: On the flip chart, write *They flew to the moon* and read the sentence out to the children. Ask them to tell you what part of the story this refers to. It may help if they spend about 30 seconds talking in pairs before answering. (The sentence describes Baby Bear's and the owl's journey to the moon.) Point out to the children that the words on the flip chart are not those that Jill Murphy uses and that they summarise a longer piece of text. Can the children remember how Jill Murphy does describe the journey? Look at page 22 in your copy of the book and read the text to the children before writing it on the flip chart. Which of the two sentences do the children prefer, and why? Discuss the differences. Why does Jill Murphy use repetition? (*On and on* and *up and up* suggest a journey over a long distance and far into space.)

Extension: Look at the uses and effects of similar repetition in other fantasy stories. For example, you could refer to page 22 of *The baby who wouldn't go to bed* where someone is *getting nearer... and nearer... and nearer*, and Max's forest that *grew and grew – and grew* in Maurice Sendak's *Where the Wild Things Are*.

Name

Date

Can I go to the moon?

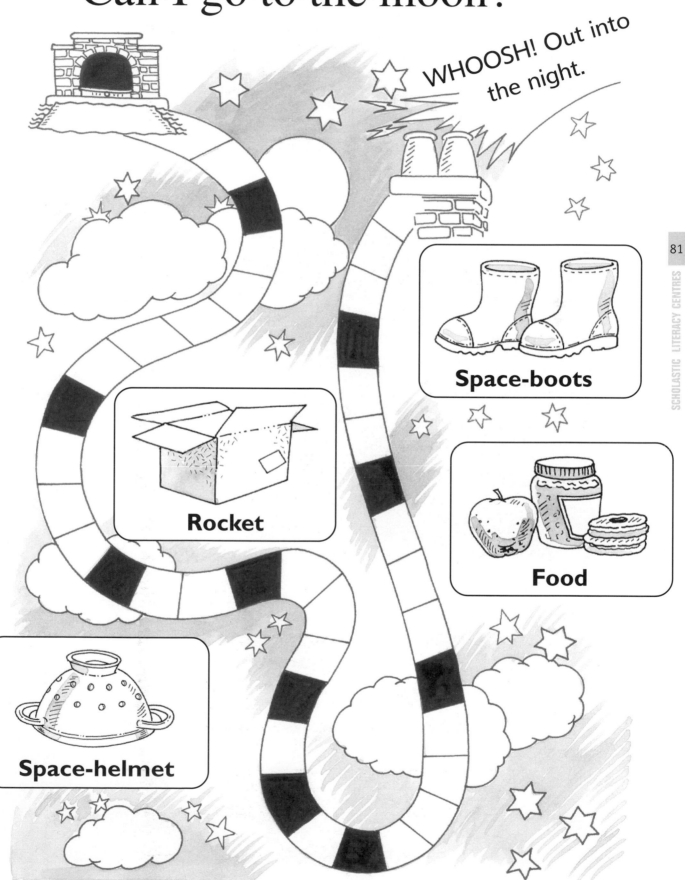

WHOOSH! Out into the night.

Space-boots

Rocket

Food

Space-helmet

SCHOLASTIC LITERACY CENTRES

Name

Date

Is it a bird?

Name

Date

A visit to the moon

SCHOLASTIC LITERACY CENTRES

owl	moon	Baby Bear
rocket	space-helmet	stars

Name   Date

Who said that?

No you can't.
It's bathtime.

There are no trees.

That's a smart rocket.
Where are you off to?

You and your stories.
Whatever next?

Goodbye. It was so
nice to meet you.

You look as if you've
been up the chimney.

Name

Date

The moon and back

Coming home

On the moon

Going to the moon

Getting ready

SCHOLASTIC LITERACY CENTRES

Name _____   Date _____

More than a box

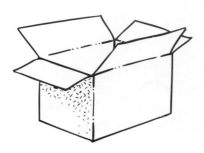

A box    can be

<u>a car</u>

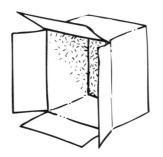

A box   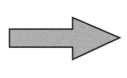 can be

_____

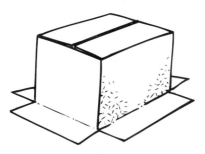

A box   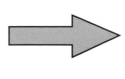 can be

_____

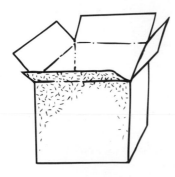

A box   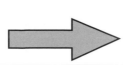 can be

_____

Name   Date

Questions, questions

Who said "I found a rocket and went to visit the moon"?	In the cupboard under the stairs.
When Baby Bear passed the aeroplane, what did some of the passengers do?	Baby Bear.
What did Baby Bear find on the mat by the front door?	They waved.
What toy did Baby Bear take with him to the moon?	A pair of space-boots.
When did Baby Bear have a bath?	His teddy.
Where did Baby Bear find the rocket?	When he came back from the moon.

Name   Date

Could you?

Could you have a bath before you go to bed?	~~No~~/Yes
Could you fly to the moon in a cardboard box?	No/Yes
Could you find boots on the mat by the front door?	No/Yes
Would you find any trees on the moon?	No/Yes
Are you likely to find a space-helmet in the kitchen?	No/Yes
Could you have a picnic on the moon with an owl?	No/Yes

Name

Date

Getting ready

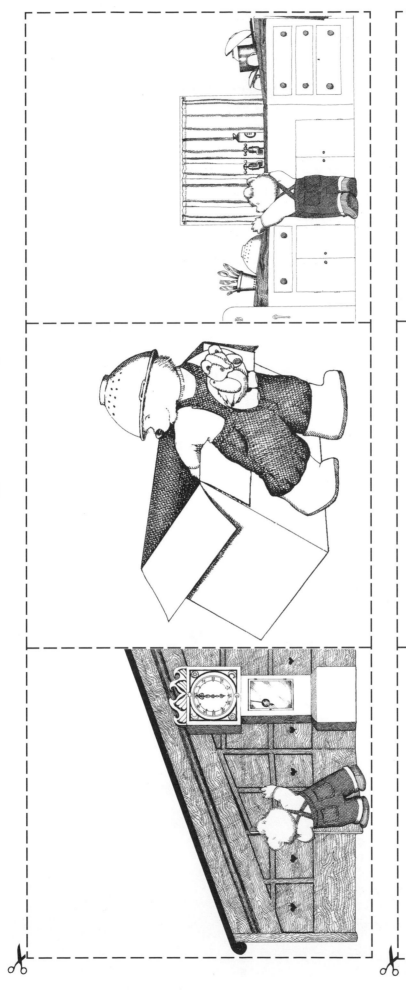

Baby Bear found a rocket in the cupboard under the stairs.

He found a space-helmet on the draining board in the kitchen, and a pair of space-boots on the mat by the door.

He packed his teddy and some food for the journey.

Name _____ Date _____

WHOOSH!

Baby Bear found a rocket _____ the cupboard

_____ the stairs.

He found a pair of space-boots on the mat _____ the

front door.

He took off _____ the chimney.

At last they landed _____ the moon.

The rain dripped _____ Baby Bear's helmet

Home went Baby Bear. Back _____ the chimney.

through up by on in under down

Rocket

Background

This is a procedural text showing how to make a model rocket. The creative construction of a model involves children in an imaginative activity which is one of the key themes in *Whatever Next!*. It also builds on the fantasy theme by developing the science-fiction element of space travel. It can be used as part of a display to go with other work on the book or as a stimulus for independent fantasy-story writing. Talking about rockets, including what they look like and how they work, will help children to understand the distinction between fact and fantasy.

The text introduces the key features of a set of instructions. These include a list of materials needed and a sequence of steps to be followed. Children can also be introduced to some of the language features (such as the use of directive sentences that begin with an imperative verb that specifies the action to be taken). You can also talk about the importance of layout and clear diagrams.

■ Read photocopiable page 93 to the children. Ask them what writing like this can be used for. (Make sure that they know it is to help the reader to make a rocket of his or her own. Draw attention to the subtitle that points this out.) Explain that the text is a set of instructions, and see if the children can think of any other situations in which instructional texts are used. For example, they may be familiar with recipes, cooking or serving instructions on food packets, 'how to play' details in games.

■ Draw attention to the layout of the text, highlighting the title, subtitle, things you'll need and the numbered list of steps. Talk about the illustrations and how they clarify the text and help the reader to understand more about what has to be done. For example, the words don't state exactly where to put the nose cone or fins, but the illustrations show where they should go. Go through some of the difficult vocabulary, such as *fin, corrugated* and *exhaust*.

■ Model the first stage of the process of making a rocket by reading through the list of what is needed. Have most of these items nearby, so that the children can take what is needed to make their rocket. Is there anything else they need which is not mentioned? (They may need brushes or spatulas for the glue. It might be a good idea to wear aprons and to cover the working area.) Explain that it is not necessary to mention these details, since it is assumed that we are prepared in this way through our previous experience of model making.

■ Tell the children to follow the instructions carefully as they are making the rocket. Get them to read and re-read each section without racing ahead or simply following the pictures. Suggest too that they read the instructions as well as *You will need* before collecting materials, as they may include important details. Ask the children to mark the sheet in places where they think more information should be provided. When they have made their rockets, ask them to evaluate the instructions. How useful were they and how could they be improved?

■ In introducing the procedural text, you will have stressed the importance of reading the instructions carefully and following them in the right order (chronological sequence). Use photocopiable page 94 to help the children to remember the stages they went through in their model making, cutting out the instructions and arranging them in the right order. Advise the children to look at the illustrations to help them organise the sequence.

CONT. . .

CONT. . .

■ Explain to the children that instructional texts often include labelled diagrams. Show the children photocopiable page 95 and demonstrate that they should label each part of the rocket diagram using the words provided.

■ Ask the children to think about how the instructional text is written. Read some of the instructions out, emphasising the verb. Explain that they are written like 'orders' with the action word – verb – at (or very near) the beginning of the sentence and addressed directly to the reader. Ask the children to go through the text picking out the verbs.

■ Ask the children to use photocopiable page 96 to plan a fantasy journey in their rocket. Encourage them to use a similar form to *Whatever Next!*, with an animal (or child) who doesn't want to go to bed, goes on a journey through space and then returns. Tell the children to read the suggested events at the bottom of the page and position them on the illustration as part of the journey plan. Point out that they may not want to use all of them and there are some 'spare' event boxes for them to include their own ideas. This activity can be used as a starting point for oral storytelling or extended writing.

ASSESSMENT NOTES

A picnic on the moon

Assessment focus: to demonstrate recall of the key events of the story; to transform a fantasy story into a list of instructions.
Resources: photocopiable page 97, writing materials.
Activity: Explain to the children that you want them to write a set of instructions on what to do if you want to have a picnic on the moon like Baby Bear did. Whilst there is some room for individual interpretation, most of the children will list the rocket (or a cardboard box), a space-helmet, space-boots, some food (this could be specified) in *You will need*; then blasting off to the moon, picking Owl up en route; landing on the moon and setting out the picnic.

What's missing?

Assessment focus: to make meaningful substitutions of words; to recall key words from the story.
Resources: photocopiable page 98, writing materials.
Activity: This is a cloze passage from the end of *Whatever Next!*. Read through the extract with the children and explain that they can fill in a space with any word that will *make sense*. In other words, they don't have to remember the exact words that Jill Murphy uses, but will need to use the same part of speech. For example, Mrs Bear could lead Baby Bear away to the *bedroom* (a noun like *bathroom* that makes sense in context). Encourage the children to read and re-read their completed sentences to make sure they do make sense. If they haven't done this sort of activity before, you could model it for them using a different extract from the story.

Rocket

Make a rocket of your very own!

You will need:	glue	glitter
a kitchen roll tube	thin card	silver paint
silver foil	corrugated card	paintbrush
scissors	coloured paper	a large sheet of black paper

1. Cover the tube with foil and glue it down. This is the body of the rocket.

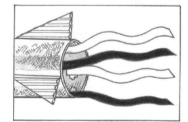

2. Make the rocket's nose cone from a circle of card. Cover this in silver foil and attach it to the foil body.

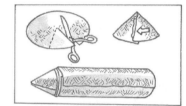

3. Cut three long triangles from corrugated card. These are the tail fins. Paint them silver. When they are dry, glue them to the rocket.

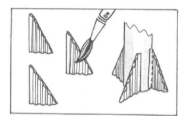

4. Use strips of coloured paper for the rocket's exhaust. Use red, blue, orange and yellow. Glue them just inside the bottom of the tube.

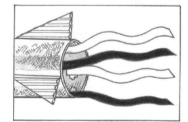

5. Make a space background from the black paper. Decorate this with silver foil and glitter for stars and planets.

6. Glue your rocket onto the space background.

Now find a good place to display your rocket picture!

fiction **yellow**

Fantasy worlds

▲ SCHOLASTIC

Name _____ Date _____

In order

Glue your rocket onto the space background.

Cover the tube with foil.

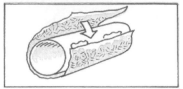

Cut out three triangles for fins and paint them silver.

Make a space background from black paper.

Make the rocket's nose cone from a circle of card.

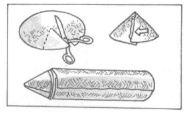

Use strips of paper for the rocket's exhaust.

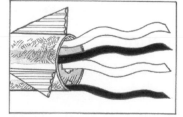

fiction **yellow**
Fantasy worlds

Name   Date

Label your rocket

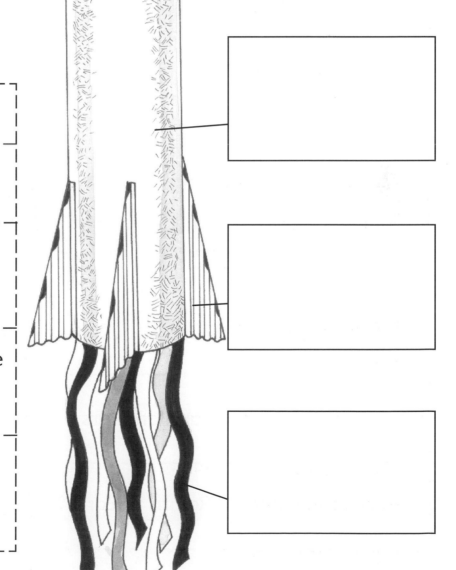

The rocket

Fins made from corrugated card

Nose cone made from a circle of card

Main body of the rocket made from a cardboard tube

Exhaust made from strips of coloured paper

Name   Date

Space journey

Meet with aliens	Fly around Saturn	
Stop on the Moon	Land on Mars	
See shooting stars	Return to Earth	

Name _____   Date _____

A picnic on the moon

You will need:

1.

2.

3.

4.

Enjoy your picnic!

fiction **yellow**
Fantasy worlds

Name _____ Date _____

What's missing?

Mrs Bear came into the room.

"Look at the *state* of you!" she gasped as she led

him away to the _____.

"Why, you look as if you've been up the

_____."

"As a matter of fact," said Baby Bear, "I *have*

been up the _____. I found a

_____ and went to visit the

_____."

Mrs Bear _____. "You and your

stories," she said. "Whatever _____?"

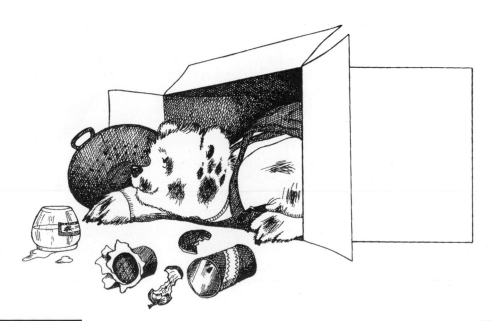

R XARGLE'S BOOK OF EARTHLETS

BY JEANNE WILLIS
ILLUSTRATED BY TONY ROSS

About the book

This humorous picture book combines the entertaining writing of Jeanne Willis with lively, fun illustrations by Tony Ross. Dr Xargle – a professorial-looking alien – teaches his alien pupils about human babies – *Earthlets*. The book takes the form of a lesson that concludes with the preparations for a school trip to Earth. In essence, the book is a parody of non-fiction writing, using the aliens' viewpoint to make fun of the routines and rituals of the everyday life of human babies. It is narrated by Dr Xargle, as the cover suggests, and 'translated' by Jeanne Willis, the author.

The book's humour is sophisticated and introduces children to some key themes in fantasy and science-fiction writing. The setting, which is not directly referred to, is a classroom on another planet; the teacher and pupils are green, furry aliens. In this way the immediate setting is familiar (although the location is imaginary) and the characters, who are a creation of fantasy, have recognisable roles and relationships. This is well illustrated by Dr Xargle's teacherly warning that the aliens must be 'very good and quiet' as they line up for the school trip to Earth at the end of the story. Both fantasy and sci-fi writing use combinations of the familiar and the imaginary to show everyday behaviour in a new light.

Dr Xargle's book of Earthlets was written in 1988. Since then, Jeanne Willis and Tony Ross have collaborated on a number of Dr Xargle sequels covering topics such as *Earth Tiggers*, *Earth Relations*, *Earth Weather* and *Earth Hounds*.

Alien points of view

Dr Xargle's Book of Earthlets draws on children's familiarity with aliens from television and films. Talking about aliens introduces an imaginative dimension to stories and children will be able to use this in their own writing. They can reflect on the way in which the film *ET*, for example, uses the alien character as a way of making the familiar unfamiliar whilst raising our interest in the possibility of other life forms. In a rather different way, children will realise how *Star Wars* and *Star Trek* stories use aliens both as allies and enemies. Other children's stories also make use of aliens. An extract from *But Martin!* by June Counsel is included on page 120 and offers interesting points for comparison and contrast. In *But Martin!* an alien visits a classroom on Earth whereas in *Dr Xargle's* book we 'visit' a classroom of aliens on their own planet.

Fact and fiction

In terms of structure, the book resembles a non-chronological report. As such, it begins by defining the topic (Earthlets). It then goes on to describe the varieties (colours), their characteristics, and their needs (feeding, changing, bathing and sleeping). Although the information is presented in a humorous way, with unusual 'alien' language, it is basically factually accurate and can be used as a starting point in modelling report writing. The book also links well with science or PSHE work on health and growth. Children could take a Dr Xargle approach to a piece of their own work, writing about familiar living things from an alien point of view.

GUIDED READING NOTES

Introduce the book by talking about the front cover, before having an initial read for enjoyment and understanding. Draw the children's attention to the title, subtitle, author and illustrator. Look carefully at the cover picture and ask the children what they think the green creature is? Is it an alien? Could it be Dr Xargle? Where is this character – is he on Earth or somewhere else? How is the setting conveyed? Talk about the scenery and the colours that Tony Ross has used. Then look at the subtitle: *An alien's view of earth babies*. Ask the children to predict what the book might be about. Discuss what sort of book it is going to be. Will it be a story like *Dreamboat Zing* or a factual book like *Bean Diary* (see page 105)?

Read the first two double-page spreads (pages 6–9, taking the very first page as page 1), up to *two long tentacles called leggies*. Ask the children what they think Dr Xargle is going to explain next. Then carry on reading the story through to the end. Ask the children what they thought about the story and which parts they liked and why. Draw attention to the fantasy element of this story. Mention the setting (on another planet) and Tony Ross's depiction of the aliens. Hold a discussion on 'aliens'. Some of the children may know a lot about the subject from television and film, and it is important to draw on this, but make sure that they are clear that most of that knowledge comes from fantasy narratives!

Conclude this session by asking the children if their initial predictions were correct. What do they think the alien children learned about Earthlets? After this discussion, see how many of Dr Xargle's Earthlet facts the children can remember. Ask them to make lists, or make a record together as a shared writing activity. (For example, Earthlets are one of four colours, they have one head, two eyes, and so on.)

After reading the book all the way through, focus on the front cover and particularly the character of Dr Xargle. Talk about his physical appearance and ask the children to describe him. What does he look like? What colour is he? What is he wearing? What kind of book is he carrying? Look closely at the baby poster propped against a rock. Talk about the image of the baby, its dummy and the arrows. How would Dr Xargle use a poster like that? The children should be able to relate this diagram to other posters and information texts they have seen. Establish what *Translated into Human* means. This discussion will help the children to understand that the book takes the form of a lesson taught by an alien teacher to a class of aliens.

Now ask the children to look at page 28, and read *That is the end of today's lesson* together. Look closely at the illustration and make sure the children can identify Dr Xargle as the teacher, the audience as alien pupils, the stage, and the teddy as a teaching prop. Remind the children that reading the first part of the book is like being one of the aliens listening to Dr Xargle's lesson.

Re-read the book, stopping at page 11 (the baby in the snow). Ask the children who they think is telling the story (remind them that it is only *translated* by Jeanne Willis!). Look back at the first double-page spread. Who is saying *'Good morning, class'*? Reinforce the idea that reading the story reproduces what it is like being an alien listening to Dr Xargle's lesson.

Now discuss what sort of children are in Dr Xargle's class. You may find it useful to refer to pages 28–9 at this point. In the earlier parts of the book, we can only imagine what Dr Xargle's audience is like. The illustrations on these pages indicate that the class is made up of creatures who look similar to Dr Xargle. Encourage the children to describe these alien school children and suggest how they

might act in the classroom and playground.

What are Earthlets, and why would Dr Xargle's class want to learn about them? Establish what Dr Xargle knows about Earthlets and encourage the children to consider how he might have found this out. Perhaps he has visited Earth to study Earth babies himself. Ask the children to examine the detail of his lesson. Is he always right about what he says? Do the group think that the information Dr Xargle has given the alien children will be helpful when they visit Earth for the first time and see real Earth babies?

Read from page 8 to page 27, reminding the children that this is the main part of Dr Xargle's lesson, and ask if Dr Xargle has his facts right. Help the children to discuss this with specific reference to the text. For instance, you might say *I think Dr Xargle is right about the colours, because children do have different skin colours. On page 8 it says 'They come in four colours. Pink, brown, black or yellow... but not green' and that's true.* The children can then express their own

opinions about Dr Xargle's lesson in a similar way.

Now talk about the language that Dr Xargle uses to explain about the Earthlets. His facts may be right, but the vocabulary is not what we would normally use. Focus on his use of the term *Earthlets*, comparing it with other words with the *-let* suffix. For example, it is used to describe animal young such as piglets and eaglets, as well as small inanimate objects like booklets, anklets and eyelets. You could extend this discussion by making a collection of *-let* words. Read page 14 as another example of Dr Xargle's unusual terminology, encouraging the children to point out the unusual terms (*fangs* for teeth and *hole in their face* instead of mouth). Think and talk about why Dr Xargle does this. Is it because he doesn't know the correct word himself or because he is trying to explain Earthlets to those who have never seen them before, and in terms that they can understand?

Review the book together. Begin by asking the children to tell you what they liked about the book and what they would say to recommend it to

CONT. . .

CONT. . .

other children. Explain that if they wrote these opinions and suggestions down it would be called a review. Explain that the back cover shows some extracts from reviews other people have written, and read the first one. Ask the children what they think of this review. Is *Dr Xargle's Book of Earthlets* really a book from another solar system? But, is that an appropriate way to refer to it? What does Bill Tidy mean when he describes himself as *a father of three Earthlets*? Now read the second review. Can the children remember who the people referred to are? (Jeanne Willis is the author, Tony Ross the illustrator.) What words are used in the *Guardian* review to sum up the story? Is *space creatures being taught about human babies* a good way of

describing the book? Read the other reviews to the children. Point out the phrase *inspired paintings bristle with out-of-this-world colour*. What does this mean and do the children agree? Discuss the different ways in which reviewers indicate that this is a humorous story (*funny book; wonderful idea; will delight; amusing*). Ask the children to think of brief descriptions like those of their own and then think about what else they might write in a review of the book. These ideas can be used in a follow-up activity involving shared or independent writing.

Re-read pages 28–30 to begin thinking about the ending. Discuss what is happening in the illustrations and talk about the school trip. Ask the children to compare this with their own school trips. What are the similarities and differences? (For instance, children may need to remember waterproof clothes and packed lunch for a school trip, but they are unlikely to need disguises! Dr Xargle, like many teachers, insists that the children are *very good and quiet* on the trip, and the aliens line up to board their

spaceship as children might to board their coach at the beginning of an outing.)

Talk about why the aliens have to put on disguises. Where is Dr Xargle taking his class and why? Ask the children to contemplate the alien children's journey to Earth. How long might it take and what would it be like on the spaceship? What do the children think will happen when the aliens visit the families on Earth? What will they be expected to do? Will they spend time with an Earth baby, taking notes and making sketches? Again, compare it to your school visits or field trips.

Encourage the children to imagine the return trip and think about what Dr Xargle will ask his class to do on their return. Will he ask them to write a report about what they did and what they have learned? Will he be asking them to write thank-you letters (or e-mails) to the host families on Earth? Perhaps when they are older the Earthlets may wish to visit the aliens. Would the children in the group like to visit aliens on another planet?

ACTIVITY NOTES

Into Human

Objectives: to examine the creative use of language in the story; to extend and develop vocabulary choices.

Resources: photocopiable page 108, writing materials. For the extension – copies of *Dr Xargle's Book of Earthlets*.

Activity: Explain that although the author (Jeanne Willis) has translated Dr Xargle's book into Human, you think it needs a little more work to turn it into everyday English so that everyone can understand it. So, the children's task is to translate what Dr Xargle says into correct English. Look at the first speech bubble on the photocopiable sheet, in which Dr Xargle says *Earthlets have no fangs at birth*. Ask the children how to improve this. Underline the words *Earthlets* and *fangs* and write *Babies have no teeth at birth*. Ask the children to complete the rest of the sheet independently.

Extension: Children could find more of Dr Xargle's terms to be translated.

Dr Xargle's next book

Objectives: to use the style of the story in their own writing; to explore and develop the themes introduced in the book.

Resources: photocopiable page 109, copies of *Dr Xargle's Book of Earthlets*, writing materials, flip chart or board.

Activity: Look at page 9 from Dr Xargle's lesson as a starting point for guided writing. Talk about how simple, everyday ideas are explained by Dr Xargle so that the aliens can understand them. Arms and legs are referred to as *tentacles*. Fingers are called *pheelers*, as this relates to what the alien children know from their own lives. You can develop this idea to include the toddler stage (learning to walk, playing with more sophisticated toys, going to nursery and so on), imagining that Dr Xargle is writing the next volume in the series of information books about humans. For example, you might begin with *When they are older, Earthlets begin to move around on their long tentacles*. Show the children the photocopiable sheet and explain that it shows a diagram of Earth children that Dr Xargle might use. Make a few suggestions first (such as trainers as *leggie-wraps*, a hairbrush as a *fur-claw*), then encourage the children to brainstorm names for other objects and items of clothing before they start recording their ideas. Ask them to label the picture using Dr Xargle language.

Extension: These new ideas for Dr Xargle's next lesson could then be written up in a similar style to Jeanne Willis's text. It could begin with *Today we are going to learn more about Earthlets...* You could split the task by asking each child to describe one or two items, then combine these as a group or class book.

Taking note

Objectives: to investigate the use of fantasy characters and settings in the story; to encourage close reading of visual images in picture books; to develop note-taking techniques.

Resources: copies of *Dr Xargle's Book of Earthlets*, large sheet of paper, writing and drawing materials.

103

SCHOLASTIC LITERACY CENTRES

Activity: This activity is based on a re-reading of *Dr Xargle's Book of Earthlets* and making notes. Before re-reading, draw the outline of a house on the paper. Make it large enough to write or draw on the inside, but leave plenty of room around the outside. Use this to keep a record of *who* is in the story (character) and *where* things take place (setting). Characters and objects that directly relate to life on Earth will be noted inside the house; those related to Dr Xargle's world will be recorded outside the house. Explain this to the children and begin by reading the cover – write *Dr Xargle* and *on his planet* outside the house. Later on, the words *granny*, *baby*, *daddy* and so on can be added (inside the house). Sketches could also be used. Note how most of this information is conveyed through Tony Ross's illustrations. Ask the children how they know that Dr Xargle is on another planet. (We understand this by inference from the pictures, our knowledge of other stories about aliens and the references to the visit to *planet Earth* and the spaceship in the final pages.)

Extension: Ask the children if the same baby and family are used throughout the illustrations (Dr Xargle's reference pictures and diagrams). This involves looking closely at the pictures and being aware that at least some of the text is in a continuous sequence (for example, the information about bathing).

Earthlets in order

Objectives: to sequence fantasy explanations in a logical order; to identify the beginning, middle and end of Dr Xargle's lesson.

Resources: photocopiable page 110, scissors, glue, paper.

Activity: Begin by reminding the children that Dr Xargle is giving a lesson to the young aliens. He begins by saying *'Good morning'* to the class and ends by preparing them for their school trip to Earth. Explain to the children that they should cut out the pictures and put them in the order that they occurred during the lesson. Then they will have to match the correct caption to each picture. This will help them to appreciate the structure of the book. You may wish to explain that because the content of Dr Xargle's lesson is basically a list of facts (like a non-fiction text), the order is not particularly important and therefore harder to remember. To successfully complete this activity it is not important for the sentences from the lesson to be in the right order. However, the beginning and ending ones do need to be.

Alien school news

Objectives: to use imagination to write about events after the end of the story; to write in the recount style of a newspaper.

Resources: photocopiable page 111, copies of *Dr Xargle's Book of Earthlets*, copies of school newspapers, writing materials, flip chart or board.

Activity: Ask the children to imagine that they are in Dr Xargle's class and he has asked them to write a report of their visit to Earth for the school newspaper. Begin the session by showing the children examples of recount writing in school newspapers. Demonstrate the importance of simple factual information that highlights one or two key events and consider an example based on the book (for instance, the aliens may have been struck by the way that Earthlets are wheeled around in prams and buggies). Complete the first part of the article together, asking the children to suggest a headline and ways of completing the starter sentence. Encourage them to compare alternatives. For example, *Last Thursday we went to visit the wild wailing Earthlets in their own homes* may be more effective than *Last Thursday we went to Earth*. Continue this section, reminding the children to think of detail that will interest readers. Discuss what might be included in the rest of the report (for example, focusing on the noise that Earthlets make) and how to round off the article at the end. Advise the children to use these ideas and/or their own to complete the report independently.

Extension: This work could be used as the basis for role-play on a news story for *Alien TV*. The children can decide on the format: main news, children's news or a magazine programme (like *Blue Peter*). Items could include factual reporting from a special correspondent, interviews with alien school children and on-location reports from Earth.

Looking after Earthlets

Objective: to present information from the fantasy story in the form of a factual advice sheet.

Resources: photocopiable page 112, copies of *Dr Xargle's Book of Earthlets*, writing materials, a collection of advice leaflets and information posters.

Activity: Discuss the purpose of the leaflets and posters with the children. Read some of them through and examine their layout and style features. Explain to the children that they are going to design an advice leaflet using the information from *Dr Xargle's Book of Earthlets*. Look at the subheadings and illustrations on the photocopiable sheet. Work on a statement for the first section together. You could either use words from the book (for example, *They must be wrapped in the hairdo of a sheep*) or everyday English (*They need to wear warm clothes*).

Contents page

Objectives: to develop the idea of sequence in the story; to develop an understanding of referencing using a contents page.

Resources: photocopiable page 113, copies of *Dr Xargle's Book of* Earthlets, a reference book with a contents page, paper, writing materials, flip chart or board.

Activity: Remind the children of their guided reading work in which you discussed the book's genre (see page 100). Emphasise that it is a fantasy that draws on our understanding of factual books and that the book has a 'standard' story structure of beginning, middle and end. Use the reference book, such as Monica Hughes's *Discovery World: Bean Diary* series (Heinemann), and use the contents page to illustrate how we can use this to find the information we need in the book. Draw attention to the fact that the page number listed in the contents refers to the first page of each section. Explain to the children that they are going to create a contents page for *Dr Xargle's Book of Earthlets*. Read out the list of contents topics and work together to put them in approximate (if not exact) order on the flip chart. Work through the first example with the children. The first information we learn is about *Appearance*. Check that the children understand the word and look in the book together to locate information on this. You might start with the information on page 9,

105

SCHOLASTIC LITERACY CENTRES

but ask the children if there is any information on appearance before this (page 8). Check again that there is nothing before this. Write *8* next to *Appearance*, explaining that this is the first page of this section of information. Make sure the children understand how to complete the sheet before they begin to work independently and advise them to work on scrap paper until they are happy with their order and page numbers, before transferring the details to the photocopiable sheet.

Extension: When the children have completed the activity, they can work in pairs to check each other's contents by choosing a topic, locating the page given and making sure that the information starts there.

Please sir!

Objectives: to empathise with the aliens in Dr Xargle's class; to use imagination to develop ideas presented in the story.

Resources: photocopiable page 114, copies of *Dr Xargle's Book of Earthlets*, writing materials, flip chart or board.

Activity: Show the children the picture on page 28. Ask them to point to Dr Xargle and to the alien pupils in his class. Explain to the group that they are going to imagine that they are the alien children and that they want to ask Dr Xargle some questions. Now look at the photocopiable sheet. Encourage the children to think of questions about Earthlets that the aliens might ask, for example *How heavy are they? How do their parents take them outside? Where do they go? How big do they grow?* Note some of these on the flip chart and draw attention to the question word (starting with a capital letter) at the beginning and the question mark at the end. Ask the children to fill in the empty speech bubbles with questions. These will form the basis of Dr Xargle's responses in the next activity.

Dr Xargle's answers

Objective: to build on knowledge of Dr Xargle's character and way of speaking.

Resources: photocopiable page 115, completed photocopiable page 114, copies of *Dr Xargle's Book of Earthlets*, writing materials.

Activity: Ask the children to read the four questions they wrote in 'Please sir!' and now to think about providing answers for them as Dr Xargle would. Encourage them to look through the book to remind themselves of the way Dr Xargle presents his facts. Tell the children to use short factual answers in the style of Dr Xargle and also use his vocabulary. Remind them of typical statements, such as *Earthlets have no fangs at birth* and *They are placed in plastic capsules*.

Extension: Children could work in pairs to generate more questions for Dr Xargle. They could then take on the roles of alien pupil and Dr Xargle, with Dr Xargle improvising answers.

Earthlet dictionary

Objectives: to practise dictionary skills by providing definitions of simple words from the story; to understand alphabetical order.

Resources: photocopiable page 116, copies of *Dr Xargle's Book of Earthlets*, dictionaries, writing materials.

Activity: Show the children the dictionary and read one of the definitions together. Demonstrate how dictionary entries are in alphabetical order and discuss how this makes the words we need to look up easy to find. Read the first entry on the photocopiable sheet (*beddybyes*) and follow the line that joins it to its definition. Discuss the next entry (*claws*) and its definition. Show the children how they can join the entry to the definition with a line. Ask the children to read the rest of the headwords, noticing they are in alphabetical order, and then match them up with their definitions.

Plug the gaps

Objective: to use contextual knowledge and reading skills to complete gaps in the text.

Resources: photocopiable page 117, writing materials.

Activity: If the children haven't done this sort of activity before, go through it together. The most important point is that the word put in the gap helps the text to make sense. So, if the children use the word *loud* to make *Earthlets can be recognised by their loud cry* (rather than the word *fierce* as used in the book), this is quite acceptable. Encourage the children to re-read each sentence after they have added the words to check that it makes sense. They can then think about it again and correct it if necessary. When they have completed the activity, you might want to compare it with the book, but talk about the effect of different word choices rather than emphasising right and wrong. It's possible that children will improve on Jeanne Willis's text!

Dr Xargle's planet

Objectives: to look closely at illustrative detail related to the fantasy setting; to describe a fantasy setting.

Resources: copies of *Dr Xargle's Book of Earthlets*, paper, writing and drawing materials, board or flip chart.

Activity: Together, study the illustrations of Dr Xargle's planet carefully. This will mean looking at the front cover, page 29 and page 30. Advise the children to look at the colours and the mountainous features of the landscape. They will also notice the clouds, rocks, three moons, four suns, and a ringed planet in another part of the sky. Write up these key words on the flip chart. Ask the children to use all of this information to draw a picture of the alien planet's landscape and label the significant features. Advise them to use different reds, pinks, browns and oranges. Underneath the picture, ask the children to write a brief description, including the words they used in their labels.

Name _____

Date _____

Into Human

Earthlets have no fangs at birth.

They are placed in plastic capsules with warm water and a yellow floating bird.

Earthlets grow fur on their heads.

Date

Name

Dr Xargle's next book

fur-claw

Name   Date

Earthlets in order

| They must be wrapped in the hairdo of a sheep. | Today we are going to learn about Earthlets. |
| Earthlets grow fur on their heads but not enough to keep them warm. | That is the end of today's lesson. |

Name _____   Date _____

Alien school news

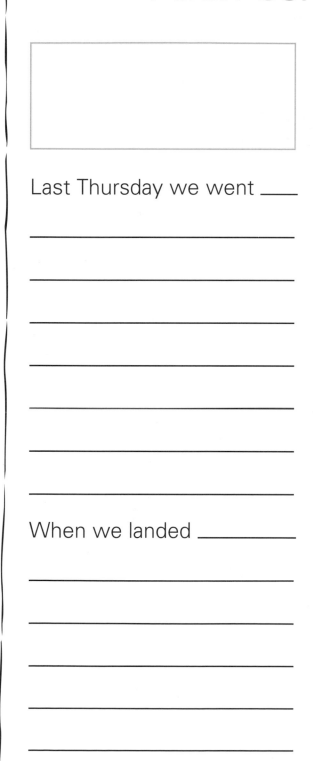

Last Thursday we went ____

_____

_____

_____

_____

_____

_____

When we landed ____

_____

_____

_____

_____

Putting on our disguises for
the Earth visit

_____

_____

_____

We got back at _____

_____

_____

_____

_____

_____

Name

Date

Looking after Earthlets

Keeping warm

Feeding

Changing

Bathing

Playing

Sleeping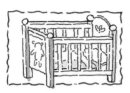

Name   Date

Contents page

Sleeping	Getting dirty	Appearance	Crying
Feeding	Cleaning	Fangs	Fur

Contents

Sections   **Page**

1. _____   _____

2. _____   _____

3. _____   _____

4. _____   _____

5. _____   _____

6. _____   _____

7. _____   _____

8. _____   _____

SCHOLASTIC LITERACY CENTRES

Name

Date

Please sir!

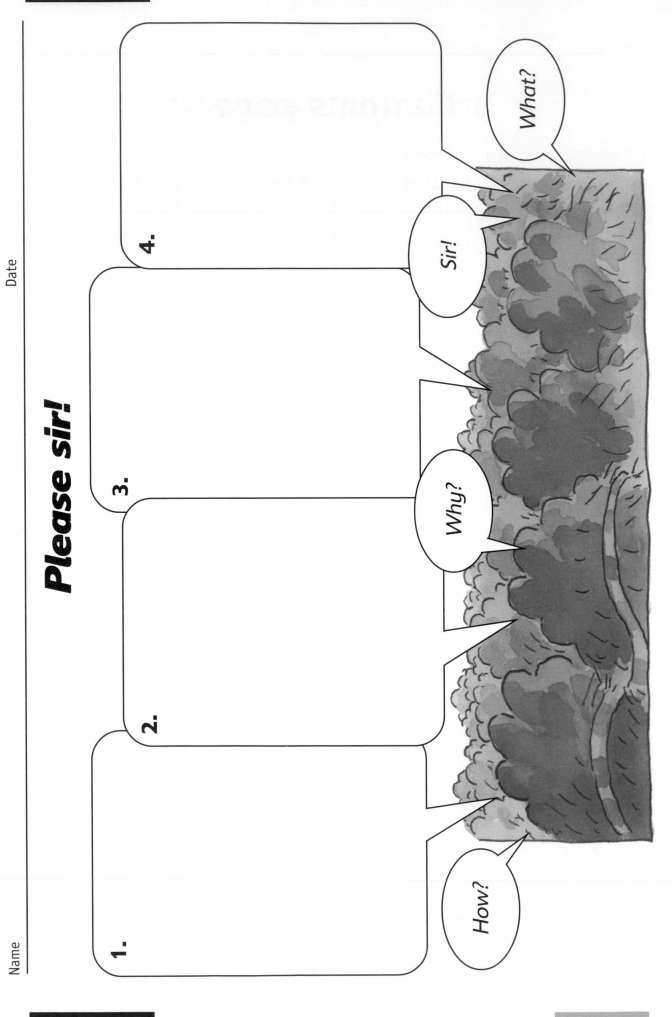

1.

2.

3.

4.

How?

Why?

Sir!

What?

Name _____ Date _____

Dr Xargle's answers

1.

2.

3.

4.

Name   Date

Earthlet dictionary

beddybyes	food made from the egg of a hen mangled with a prong
claws	a small bear that lives in beddybyes
eggmangle	a swinging box with soft lining
fur	hole in the face for food
grannies	used to frighten off wild beasts
hairdo of sheep	Earthlets grow *some* on their heads
leggies	used by Grannies to make Earthlet wrappers
mouth	very old Earthlings who unravel sheep
Teddy	the Earthlets' long tentacles

Name _____ Date _____

Plug the gaps

Earthlets can be recognised by their _____

cry, "WAAAAAAA!" To stop them doing

_____, the Earthling daddy picks them up

_____ flings them into the atmosphere.

Then _____ tries to catch them. If they

_____ cry, the Earthling mummy pulls

their _____ one by one and says "This

_____ piggy went to market" until the

_____ makes a "hee

hee" noise. If _____

still cry, they are sent to

_____ place called

beddybyes.

But Martin!

Background

This extract is from a popular picture book with a number of similarities to the Dr Xargle story. It builds on the fantasy theme by introducing a science-fiction character into a familiar setting. In *But Martin!* an alien visits Earth and joins in everyday school life. The story introduces children from a variety of ethnic backgrounds (another similarity with *Dr Xargle's Book of Earthlets*) as they take part in familiar classroom activities. Martin is different in quite significant ways and his special abilities (floating in mid-air, vanishing and moving through solid walls) contrast with the 'ordinariness' of his classmates. The story ends with children going home by bicycle, by bus and on foot. Martin leaves in his flying saucer! The extract describes the school children and Martin in a way that compares with page 8 of *Dr Xargle's Book of Earthlets*.

■ Draw attention to the title of the extract. (The children may already be familiar with the story.) Then read photocopiable page 120 together and discuss what it is about. The first line gives the setting or context – the first morning at school after a holiday – and the others describe the characters – ordinary school children, except Martin. How many children are described and what are their names? Who is Martin and how is he different? Ask the children how they would react if they came back after a holiday and someone like Martin had joined the class.

■ Discuss the language features in the extract. Can the children see any patterns? Point out the repeated *down*. Not only does the word describe what the children looked like but also how they felt on their first day back at school. Look at the second section and again ask the children to identify the language pattern. Each child's face is described with two adjectives – one giving the shape of the face and the other its colour. Follow up this discussion with photocopiable page 121. Using the extra text for reference, ask the children to match the descriptions to the name, cutting out all the strips and pasting the pairs together onto the grid provided, in order if they can.

■ Talk about the different methods that June Counsel uses to convey how the children feel on the first morning of school. She describes their faces and movements as a way of capturing their emotions. What are these emotions? Ask the children in the group how they feel on the first morning back at school after a holiday. Ask one or two children to mime arriving at school and to use facial expressions to indicate how they feel. As a guided writing activity, create some sentences similar to those in the extract, using the names of the children in the group. Go on to talk about how the children in *But Martin!* might have felt after Martin joined their class. Would his visit have made the first day at school more enjoyable? What sort of things would they talk about when they got home? Explain that later in the story we find out that Martin can do all sorts of unexpected things like float, vanish, move through walls and work out difficult maths in his head. Encourage the children to add their own ideas of what he might be able to do. On photocopiable page 122, and using the extract as a model, ask the children to write another section for *But Martin!*, describing how the children look and feel after their first day at school.

■ How would the children in the group feel if they had an alien visitor? Encourage them to think of how the alien might arrive, what it might do in school and how it would leave. Ask the children to make concertina books that tell the story of an alien visitor to the school. Alternatively, ask them to imagine what it would be like to have an alien teacher. Give them the scenario that you are away for the day and the class is taught by an alien supply teacher!

■ Later in the story, Martin vanishes briefly. All we know from the extract is that Martin is green. Using their general knowledge of aliens together with ideas from *Dr Xargle's Book of Earthlets*, ask the children to design a poster on photocopiable page 123 to help find him. Tell them to write a brief description of his distinguishing features and where he was last seen, and to draw his picture in the frame.

assessment

ASSESSMENT NOTES

What about Earthlets?

Assessment focus: to recall details about Earthlets from Dr Xargle's lesson; to recall specific vocabulary used in the book.
Resources: photocopiable page 124, writing materials.
Activity: Before starting this activity, explain to the children that you want to know what they can remember from *Dr Xargle's Book of Earthlets*. See if they can recall six pieces of information that Dr Xargle gives about Earthlets. Ask the children if they can remember as well some of the 'special' words that Dr Xargle uses and to include these in their captions on the sheet. As an example, remind them that Dr Xargle refers to teeth as *fangs*.

Dr Xargle's information

Assessment focus: to demonstrate accurate recall of detail in the story; to respond to the text by evaluating Dr Xargle's expertise.
Resources: photocopiable page 125, writing materials, flip chart or board.
Activity: Explain to the children that the sheet shows some sentences about the book, but that an important fact is wrong each time. Look at the first sentence as an example and demonstrate how to complete the sheet. Read the sentence together carefully and ask the children to think about what is wrong with it. Why is it not accurate? Decide on an answer (in this case, there are two possible: he could be talking *about* the Earthlets or to the *aliens*) and draw a line through the word to cross it out. Then write the correct word above it. Before asking the children to complete the rest of the sheet, tell them that, for the second part of the activity, you want them to consider how much Dr Xargle knows about Earthlets. Are there any important details he has left out? How true is the information he gives his class? Tell them to use their recall of the book when giving reasons in their response.

SCHOLASTIC LITERACY CENTRES

120

But Martin!

That first morning back at school
Lee's lips turned down
Lloyd's head hung down
Billy's brows drew down
And Angela's tears fell down
but that was before they found
MARTIN!

Lee's face was smooth and golden
Lloyd's face was round and brown
Billy's face was square and red
And Angela's face was long and white
but Martin's face was
GREEN!

June Counsel

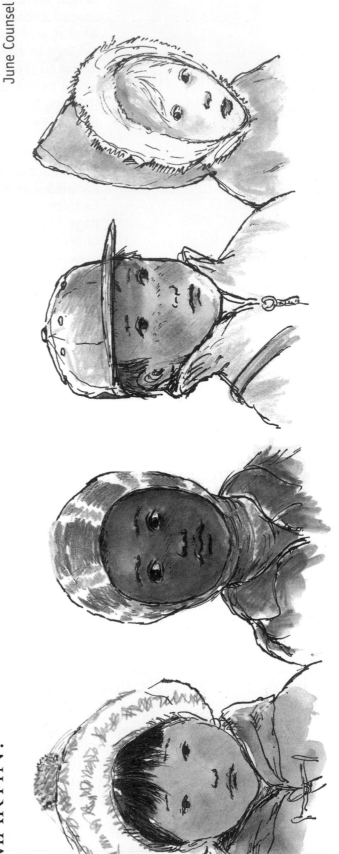

Name _____ Date _____

The faces

Angela's face was	green.
Lloyd's face was	smooth and golden.
Billy's face was	long and white.
Lee's face was	square and red.
Martin's face was	round and brown.

fiction **yellow**

Fantasy worlds

SCHOLASTIC

Name _____   Date _____

How does it feel?

After that first day at school...

Lee _____

_____

Lloyd _____

_____

Billy _____

_____

And Angela _____

_____

but Martin

was gone.

Name _____   Date _____

LOST: ALIEN

Martin looks like... _____

_____

_____

_____

Martin was last seen... _____

_____

_____

124

Date

Name

What about Earthlets?

Name   Date

Dr Xargle's information

about

Dr Xargle is talking ~~to~~ the Earthlets.

The aliens in the book are blue.

At the end of the book, the aliens visit Earth on a train.

Dr Xargle says that Earthlings eat eggmash.

Earthlings' beds are called 'plastic boats'.

Dr Xargle thinks that mummy and daddy are wild beasts.

I think Dr Xargle knows **everything** / **not much** about

Earthlets, because

The Gruffalo

Julia Donaldson and Axel Scheffler

This book draws on traditional tales and animal stories with a fantasy element. The central character is a vulnerable-looking mouse who takes a walk through a *deep dark wood*. As in traditional tales like 'The Gingerbread Man' and 'The Runaway Pancake', the mouse meets a succession of characters who want to eat him. Each one is frightened off by the mention of an imaginary monster with *terrible tusks and terrible claws* called a gruffalo. Just as the mouse escapes from the last animal – a snake – he encounters a real gruffalo! The Gruffalo wants to eat him up too, but the cunning mouse explains that he is *the scariest creature in this wood* and demonstrates this by retracing his steps. Finally, the mouse threatens to eat the Gruffalo who runs away in fright!

   This is a patterned text with repetitive phrases and plenty of surprises. It is written in a lively style, using rhyming couplets, and the Gruffalo is a good example of a fantasy monster, with interesting parallels with Maurice Sendak's classic *Where the Wild Things Are*.

■ After reading the story, ask the children if they can remember what the Gruffalo looks like and how he is described in the text. Explain that he is an imaginary *fantasy* animal. Write out the rhymes the mouse uses when describing him and learn to say them together.

■ Organise some prediction work based on the second part of the story, in which the mouse takes the Gruffalo to meet the animals. Begin by looking at some examples – *I hear a hiss in the leaves ahead*. What animal could it be? Turn the page to confirm the guess.

■ Talk about the use of exclamation marks in *The Gruffalo* (for example, *Roasted fox! I'm off!*) and explain that these are all expressions of surprise. Now look at how they are used in the second part of the story (*Oh crumbs! Amazing!* and so on). Extend this by brainstorming alternative exclamations that the creatures could say.

■ Read an extract from the text, exaggerating the rhyming words and rhythm of the rhyming couplets, and ask the children what they notice. Write an example of the words and ask the children to help you find the rhyming words to underline. Find rhymes with shared spelling, such as *claws* and *jaws*, and compare these with words that sound the same (rhyme) but have different spelling patterns, for example *said* and *fled*.

■ Talk about the 'fantasy' meals in the story (for example, *roasted fox, owl ice cream, scrambled snake* and *gruffalo crumble*). Use these in a shared writing session to start a group or class menu of fantasy foods. Build on this by adding other animal dishes.

Where the Wild Things Are

Maurice Sendak

This classic picture book was first published in 1963 and charts the fantasy adventures of Max. The story begins in a familiar setting, showing Max at home in a mischievous mood, wearing his wolf suit. He is sent to bed without any supper and then escapes from everyday reality to become *king of all wild things*. After his fantasy adventures with the wild things he eventually returns home to eat his supper.

Like *The baby who wouldn't go to bed*, Sendak's story follows a simple flight of fantasy structure, beginning and ending with the familiar night-time domestic setting. The middle part of the story explores Max's fantasy, triggered by his mother calling him *WILD THING*, as he acts out or imagines a journey to where the wild things are.

■ Look at the story structure of the book. Draw three large boxes in a line on a flip chart or board with arrows connecting them. Label them *the beginning*, *the middle* and *the end*. Ask the children to tell you about *who* is shown at the beginning of the story, *where* they are, and *what* they are doing. Make short notes about this inside the first box. Now repeat this process for the remaining two sections. Go on to discuss the fantasy element of the story. Does this remind the children of any other stories they have read?

■ Study one of the double-page spreads that show the wild things, covering the text. Ask the children if they can remember how the author describes them. (They have *terrible roars, terrible teeth, terrible eyes* and *terrible claws*.) Ask the children to work in pairs and think of and talk about their own descriptions for the wild things. Now choose one of the wild things, draw a rough outline of its figure and use the children's ideas to create a labelled diagram of a fantasy monster.

■ Discuss Max's actions at the beginning of the story. Encourage the children to look closely at the pictures that show Max at home. What sorts of mischief does he make? How might his mother feel and how does she react? Is Max really a wild thing? Now look closely at the illustration at the end of the book where Max re-enters his bedroom. What is Max thinking? How does he feel? Work with the children to compose a thought bubble to accompany this picture. Extend this activity by comparing this illustration with one that shows Max in his role as the king of all wild things.

■ Organise some drama activities based on the book. Choose a child to put in the hot seat as Max, encouraging the other children to ask questions related to the story (such as *Why did you get sent to your room? What did you do when you reached the island?*) and others that extend knowledge of the story (*What was happening before the story started? Who bought the wolf suit for you?* and so on). You could also ask two children to improvise a telephone conversation between Max (when he is on the island) and his mother at home.

Let the Lynx Come In

Jonathan London and Patrick Benson

This picture book uses the familiar flight of fantasy structure, which begins and ends in a 'real' situation. Like *The baby who wouldn't go to bed* and *Where the Wild Things Are*, the young reader can identify with the central character, who in this case is a young boy. The boy and his father are staying in a log cabin in the woods. When his father falls asleep, the boy hears a scratching at the door. He goes to look and discovers that it is a lynx who then takes him on a fantasy adventure to the moon and back. He returns safely to the log cabin where his father is still asleep.

The book has a simple story structure that is brought alive by Jonathan London's lyrical writing and Patrick Benson's powerful full-page illustrations in which a smallish wild cat transforms into the awesome, beautiful Great Lynx.

■ After your first reading, talk about the story structure of the book. Represent this as a large circle on a flip chart or board. Underneath the circle, draw a simple outline of a log cabin for the beginning and end of the story. On the circle, draw arrows pointing in a clockwise direction. Ask the children to say where the story begins. Jot down any phrases they can remember about the first double-page spread (for instance, the pot-belly stove, father snoring). Ask: *What does the boy hear?* and write down the answer (scratching at the door). Carry on in this way, working your way round the circle. This representation of the story can be used for oral retellings by the children.

■ Look at the figurative language that is used to describe the lynx. When the lynx first comes in he is *still as a stone* and *quiet as an owl*. Explain to the children how you can describe something by comparing it with something else. Look out for further use of figurative language as you re-read the story. You'll notice that the Lynx's gaze is *like fire from the Northern Lights* and that he lands by the door *like a pile of snow*.

■ Re-read page 18 (beginning *In the trees*) and talk about the way the language is used here. How is the branch described? Show how Jonathan London sometimes uses two adjectives together for effective description (the *bare black branch*, the *hard northern night* and later the *big round moon*). Experiment with missing one or both of the adjectives out. Do the children prefer it the way it is written? Now focus on the verb forms in this sentence. Does the moon really tremble or roll along? This use of imagery is another way in which the author captures the scene for us.

■ Re-read the story, looking at the different ways in which the author describes how the Great Lynx moves. You could make a collection of these words, writing them on a flip chart or board as you come across them. Notice how the Great Lynx *creeps, leaps, steps,* is *stalking, climbs, lands with a pounce, crouches* and finally *bounds away*. What effect do these verbs have? You can test this out by covering them up with Post-it Notes. Try substituting, for example, *walks, jumps* or *stops*. What effect does this have on how the story reads?